THE BOOK OF GIFTS From the Pantry

T H E   B O O K   O F

GIFTS
From the Pantry

ANNETTE GRIMSDALE

Photography by RAY JOYCE

HPBooks®

ANOTHER BEST SELLING VOLUME FROM HP BOOKS®

Published by HP Books®, P.O. Box 5367, Tucson, AZ 85703 602/888–2150
ISBN: 0–89586–506–8
Library of Congress Card Number: 86–81352
1st Printing

By arrangement with Salamander Books Limited and Merehurst Press, London.

Publisher: Rick Bailey
Editorial Director: Elaine Woodard
Editors: Maureen Reynolds, Susan Tomnay, Hilary Walden, Chris Fayers
Designers: Susan Kinealy, Roger Daniels, Richard Slater, Stuart Willard
Food stylist: Jan Barnett
Photographer: Ray Joyce
Typeset by Lineage
Color separation by Fotographics Ltd, London–Hong Kong
Printed by New Interlitho S.p.A., Milan

CONTENTS

INTRODUCTION

'The art of giving presents is to give something
which others cannot buy for themselves.'
A. A. Milne.

This is a book of ideas for gifts that cannot be bought ready made in the shops. The gifts are more meaningful and therefore more welcome because of the love and thought that has gone into their preparation and into the boxing and wrapping of them. Many of these gifts will last, but some are to be eaten and enjoyed at once. Whichever type of recipe you choose for your friends or loved ones, I know they will be delighted to receive a gift uniquely yours. Happy giving!

BLUE CHEESE DRESSING

2 oz Roquefort or blue cheese, mashed
1 clove garlic, crushed
½ teaspoon dry mustard
1 egg yolk
2 tablespoons white wine vinegar
1 teaspoon salt
1 teaspoon sugar
½ teaspoon white pepper
½ cup vegetable oil

In a bowl, mix together cheese, garlic, mustard and egg yolk.

Stir in vinegar, salt, sugar and pepper.

Stir in the oil drop by drop until half of oil has been added. Then stir in oil in a steady stream. Pour into clean container. Store in refrigerator. Will keep up to 2 weeks.

Makes about 1 cup.

Green Goddess Dressing

2 anchovy fillets, drained, mashed to a paste
1 clove garlic
1 cup Mayonnaise, page 10
1 tablespoon lemon juice
1 tablespoon tarragon vinegar
2 tablespoons finely chopped green onion, white only
2 tablespoons chopped parsley
1/4 cup sour cream
Salt and pepper
2 teaspoons fresh chopped tarragon or chives, if desired

Mix anchovies with garlic and Mayonnaise.

Stir in lemon juice, vinegar, onions and parsley.

Add sour cream and taste for salt and pepper. Pour into clean container, sprinkle tarragon over top, if desired. Store, covered, in the refrigerator. Will keep up to 7 days.

Makes about 1 3/4 cups.

MAYONNAISE

3 egg yolks, room temperature
Pinch of dry mustard
½ teaspoon salt
1¼ cups olive oil, room temperature
½ teaspoon tarragon vinegar

In a medium-size bowl, combine egg yolks, mustard and salt.

Stirring with a wooden spoon add olive oil drop by drop making sure that each drop has been absorbed before adding the next. When yolks start thickening, oil can be added in a thin stream, until a third of the oil has been incorporated. Add vinegar drop by drop alternatively with remaining oil, until vinegar is incorporated.

Add any remaining oil very slowly stirring constantly. Pour into clean container, cover. Store in refrigerator up to 7 days.

Makes about 1¾ cups.

Spicy Barbecue Sauce

2 large onions, finely chopped
2 fresh chilies, finely chopped
3 cloves garlic, crushed
1 teaspoon dry mustard
1 teaspoon salt
2 teaspoons pepper
1 tablespoon packed brown sugar
1 cup tomato catsup
½ cup olive oil
⅓ cup lemon juice
2 tablespoons tarragon vinegar
1 tablespoon Tabasco sauce
2 tablespoons chili sauce
½ cup water

In a saucepan combine all ingredients except chilies.

Bring to a boil. Add chilies. Simmer 15 minutes.

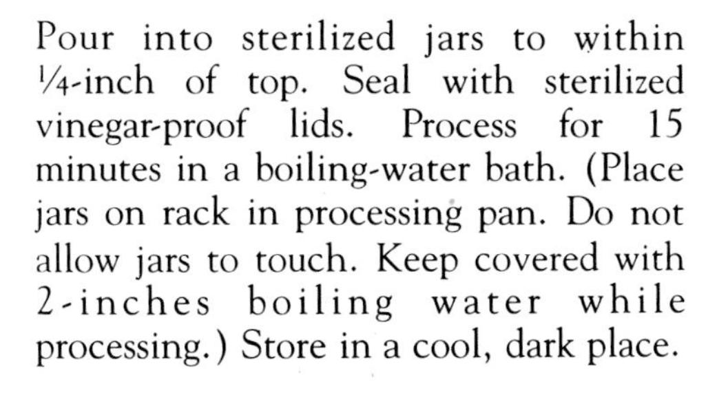

Pour into sterilized jars to within ¼-inch of top. Seal with sterilized vinegar-proof lids. Process for 15 minutes in a boiling-water bath. (Place jars on rack in processing pan. Do not allow jars to touch. Keep covered with 2-inches boiling water while processing.) Store in a cool, dark place.

Makes 3 to 3½ cups.

SALSA BOLOGNESE

2 small onions, chopped
¼ cup corn oil
1 stalk of celery, finely chopped
1 small carrot, finely chopped
½ lb. lean ground beef
Salt and freshly ground pepper
Pinch of nutmeg
½ teaspoon dried oregano
½ cup dry white wine
1 cup beef stock
2 tablespoons tomato paste

In a large heavy-bottomed saucepan or skillet fry onion in oil 2 minutes; add celery and carrot; fry until soft. Add meat and brown thoroughly.

Add salt, pepper, nutmeg and oregano. Increase heat and add white wine. Bring to a boil and allow most of the wine to evaporate.

Add beef stock and tomato paste and simmer 30 to 45 minutes. Adjust seasoning if necessary. Pour sauce into jars, seal and cool. Store in the refrigerator up to 7 days.

Makes about 3 cups.

Chili Sauce

6 medium-size onions, finely chopped
½ cup peanut oil
10 cloves garlic, chopped
1 small green pepper, chopped
2 tablespoons fresh grated gingerroot
7 ounces fresh red chilies, chopped
1½ cups tomato catsup

In a large, heavy-bottomed saucepan or skillet, gently fry onions in oil until they are soft.

Add pepper, garlic and ginger and cook two minutes more. Add chilies (leave all the seeds in if you want a very hot sauce; remove some or all for a milder sauce). Simmer about 5 minutes.

In a food processor or blender, place mixture with tomato catsup. Blend until mixture is a purée. Return to saucepan and simmer gently 15 minutes more. Pour into sterilized jars. Seal. Cool. Store in the refrigerator. Will keep up to 2 weeks.

Makes about 3 cups.

Salsa Pizzaiolo
(Neapolitan Tomato Sauce)

2 lb. fresh tomatoes
2 onions, finely chopped
2½ tablespoons corn oil
5 cloves garlic, finely chopped
1 (6 ounce) can tomato paste
¾ tablespoon fresh chopped oregano
¾ tablespoon fresh chopped basil
1 bay leaf
2 teaspoons sugar
Salt and fresh ground pepper

Peel, core and coarsely chop tomatoes.

In a large, heavy-bottomed saucepan fry onions in oil until soft.

Add garlic and cook another minute, stirring constantly (do not allow garlic to brown). Add tomatoes, tomato paste, oregano, basil, bay leaf, sugar, salt and pepper to saucepan. Bring to a boil over high heat; immediately reduce heat and simmer gently for about 30 minutes. Remove bay leaf and adjust seasoning if necessary. If you like a very smooth texture you can purée the sauce. Pour sauce into jars, seal. Store in refrigerator up to 10 days.

Makes about 6 cups.

TOMATO RELISH

3 lb. tomatoes
4 large onions, coarsely chopped
½ cup salt
2½ cups white wine vinegar
2 cups sugar
10 small red chilies (or fewer, if less spicy relish is preferred)
1 tablespoon curry powder
1 tablespoon turmeric
1½ teaspoons dry mustard
1 teaspoon cumin
1 teaspoon fenugreek
2 tablespoons all-purpose flour

Peel, core and coarsely chop tomatoes. Place in a ceramic or glass bowl, sprinkle generously with salt; cover; let stand overnight. In a large saucepan combine tomatoes, onions and vinegar. Bring to boil; simmer 10 minutes. Add sugar and chilies. Continue to cook, stirring occasionally, until sugar is dissolved. Simmer 5 minutes more.

In a small bowl combine remaining ingredients and enough cold water to form a paste. Add to simmering vegetable mixture, stirring to avoid any lumps. Simmer 1½ hours stirring occasionally.

Pour into sterilized jars. Seal with sterilized vinegar-proof lids. Process, page 11. Store in a cool, dark place. Allow to mellow 4 weeks before using.

Makes about 4 pints.

— GREEN PEPPERCORN MUSTARD —

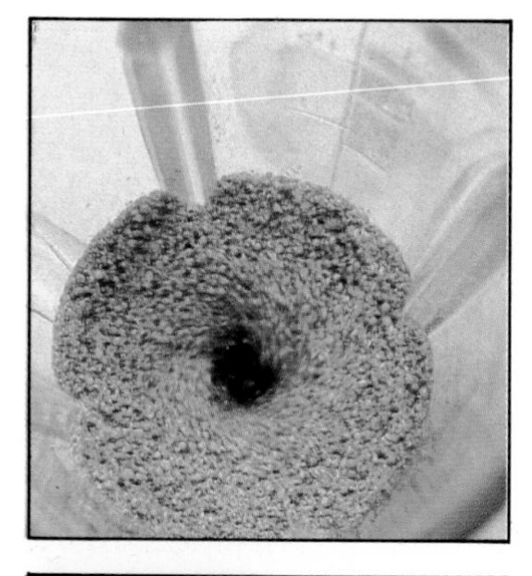

6 tablespoons white mustard seeds
3 tablespoons green peppercorns
2 tablespoons honey
¼ cup cider vinegar
1 tablespoon salt
½ teaspoon powdered nutmeg
¼ teaspoon powdered allspice

In a blender, grind mustard seeds finely. In a glass or ceramic bowl, mix together mustard powder and 3 tablespoons water, let stand 30 minutes.

In a blender, place mustard mixture, green peppercorns, honey, vinegar, salt, nutmeg and allspice. Blend ingredients until mustard acquires a grainy texture. If mixture seems too dry, add a little more water or honey.

Cover and let stand 12 hours before pouring into sterilized jars. Seal. Store in a dark place – allow to mellow 2 weeks before using. Refrigerate after opening.

Makes about 1 cup.

Horseradish Mustard

¼ cup dry mustard
2 tablespoons grated fresh horseradish
1 teaspoon salt
¼ cup white vinegar
1 tablespoon olive oil

In a food processor or blender combine all ingredients.

Process until a smooth paste is formed.

When smooth, pour into a sterilized jar and seal. Store in the refrigerator – allow to mellow 2 weeks before using.

Makes about ¾ cup.

– Hot Malt Whiskey Mustard –

¼ cup black mustard seeds
¼ cup white mustard seeds
4 tablespoons water
⅔ cup cider vinegar
⅔ cup whiskey
½ cup honey
1 tablespoon ground nutmeg
1 tablespoon salt
Add if a very grainy mustard is desired:
¼ cup black mustard seeds
¼ cup white mustard seeds

In a blender grind black and white mustard seeds.

In a glass or ceramic bowl mix together mustard powder and water; let stand 30 minutes.

Place mustard mixture, vinegar, whiskey, honey, nutmeg and salt in blender or food processor. Process until mustard acquires a grainy texture. Add more honey if ingredients look too dry. Add additional whole black and white mustard seeds if desired. Blend again, breaking down grains but still retaining a 'whole grain' appearance. Cover; let stand overnight. Moisten with more honey if mixture appears too dry. Pour into sterilized jars and seal. Store in a cool, dark place – allow to mellow 3 weeks before using. Refrigerate after opening.

Makes 2½ to 3 cups.

MIXED HERB VINEGAR

1 cup chopped mixed fresh herbs such as rosemary, oregano, fennel and basil
2 cups white wine or cider vinegar

In a wide-necked jar that herbs half-fill, place herbs and vinegar. Cover with a vinegar-proof lid. Leave in a warm place for 2 weeks; shake the jar daily.

Strain vinegar through cheesecloth. In a clean 1-pint bottle place a sprig of herbs. Pour in the vinegar. Seal with a vinegar-proof lid.

Variation:
English Herb Vinegar: Use 4 tablespoons chopped fresh sage and 6 tablespoons chopped fresh thyme in place of mixed herbs. Place a sprig of sage and a sprig of thyme in the 1-pint bottle with the strained vinegar.

Tarragon Vinegar: Use 10 tablespoons chopped tarragon in place of mixed herbs. Place a sprig of tarragon in the 1-pint bottle with strained vinegar.

FLAVORED OILS

CHILI OIL

6 small or 3 large fresh chilies
2 cups second-grade olive oil, peanut oil or corn oil

GARLIC OIL

5 garlic cloves
1 teaspoon black pepper
2 cups second- grade olive-oil, peanut oil or corn oil

If making chili oil, prick chilies with a fork or point of a small, sharp knife. Slice large chilies. If making garlic oil, peel garlic cloves.

For chili oil, place chilies in a clean bottle. Pour in oil. Seal. Allow to mellow 10 days before using. Will keep up to 2 months.

For garlic oil, place garlic, black pepper and oil in a clean bottle. Seal. Allow to mellow 10 days. Will keep up to 2 weeks.

Herb Butters

BASIL BUTTER

½ cup butter, softened
8 to 10 fresh basil leaves, minced

Beat butter and basil together until creamy. Press into a butter mold or roll into a cylinder and cover in plastic wrap. Chill until firm.

MIXED HERB BUTTER

1 cup butter, softened
1 teaspoon each of finely chopped fresh parsley, sage, oregano and rosemary

Beat butter until creamy. Add the herbs and beat again. Roll into cylinders and cover with plastic wrap, baking parchment or wax paper. Refrigerate until firm.

GARLIC BUTTER

½ cup butter
4 cloves garlic, crushed
½ teaspoon white pepper
2 tablespoons finely chopped fresh parsley

Beat butter, garlic, pepper and parsley together until creamy. Press into a butter mold. Refrigerate until firm.

HOME-CURED PICKLES

Fresh grape leaves, washed
2 lb. small pickling cucumbers, washed and trimmed
¾ cup salt
2 quarts warm water
11 cups white vinegar
½ cup sugar
2 tablespoons whole peppercorns
¾-inch piece fresh gingerroot
1 tablespoon whole allspice
1 tablespoon whole cloves
3 cloves garlic
1 tablespoon white mustard seeds
2 teaspoons powdered nutmeg

Line a large glass or ceramic bowl with grape leaves. Place cucumbers in bowl. Dissolve salt in warm water. Cool. Pour brine mixture over cucumbers. Cover with grape leaves and let stand in a cool place for about 5 days, or until cucumbers become yellow.

Combine remaining ingredients and boil 5 minutes. Strain.

Wash cucumbers and pack tightly into sterilized jars. Pour pickling vinegar over cucumbers. Seal and leave in a warm place until cucumbers turn green again. Pour vinegar into a saucepan and bring to a boil. Allow to boil 3 minutes. Pour vinegar back into jars to cover cucumbers to within ¼-inch of top. Seal with sterilized vinegar-proof lids. Process, page 11. Store in a cool, dark place – allow to mellow at least 2 weeks before using.

Makes 4 to 5 pints.

Pickled Watermelon

2 lb watermelon peel, cut into pieces to fit jars (leaving some pink on peel)
½ cup salt
2 quarts water
5 cups sugar
2½ cups cider vinegar
1 lemon, sliced
1 cinnamon stick
1 teaspoon whole black peppercorns
1 teaspoon whole allspice
1 teaspoon whole cloves

In a glass or ceramic bowl, place peel, salt and water, cover; let stand overnight.

Drain and rinse peel. Place in a large saucepan, cover with water, bring to a boil. Simmer until rind is just tender, about 3 minutes.

Bring remaining ingredients to a boil and simmer 15 minutes. Strain liquid. Add watermelon peel and simmer until rind becomes translucent; drain. Pack rind tightly into sterilized jars. Pour syrup to within ¼-inch of top. Seal with sterilized vinegar-proof lids. Process 15 minutes in boiling-water bath, for pint containers. (Place jars on rack in processing pan. Do not allow to touch. Keep covered with 2 inches of boiling water while processing.) Store in cool, dark place, allow to mellow at least one month before using.

Makes 6 pints.

— PICKLED MIXED VEGETABLES —

1 head cauliflower
4 carrots
4 celery sticks
2 green peppers
1 each red and yellow peppers
¾ cup olives
1 quart white vinegar
1¼ cups olive oil
½ cup sugar
2 teaspoons salt
½ teaspoon pepper
1 teaspoon dried oregano

Cut cauliflower into flowerets. Peel carrots and cut into even-sized sticks. String celery, cut into sticks. Seed peppers and cut into strips.

In a large enamel saucepan, combine vegetables, olives, vinegar, oil, sugar, salt, pepper and oregano. Bring to a boil, stirring to dissolve sugar. Cover and simmer 5 minutes. Uncover and let vegetables cool in the liquid.

Spoon the vegetables into sterilized jars. Bring liquid to boil and pour over vegetables to within ½-inch of top of jars. Seal with sterilized vinegar-proof lids. Process 20 minutes in boiling-water bath for 1-pint containers. (Place jars on rack in processing pan. Do not allow jars to touch. Keep covered with 2-inches boiling water while processing.) Store in a cool, dark place — allow to mellow 2 months before using.

Makes about 3 quarts.

PICKLED ONIONS

2½ lb. small white boiling onions
¾ cup coarse salt
2 quarts white vinegar
¼ cup pickling spice, tied together in bag made from several layers of cheese cloth
2¼ cups sugar

Cover onions with boiling water. Let stand 2 minutes. Drain and dip in cold water. Peel. In a large ceramic bowl mix together onions and salt. Just cover with cold water. Cover and refrigerate. Boil vinegar, sugar and pickling spice bag for 5 minutes. Allow spices to cool in vinegar for 2 to 3 hours. Discard spice bag.

In sterilized jars to within ¼-inch of top, pack onions firmly. Pour vinegar over onions and seal with sterilized lids.

Process 30 minutes in boiling-water bath for pint containers. (Place jars on rack in processing pan. Do not allow jars to touch. Keep covered with 2 inches boiling water while processing.) Store in cool, dark place – allow to mellow 3 months before using.

Makes 5 pints.

Pickled Mushrooms

2 lb. small fresh mushrooms, rinsed
2½ cups white wine vinegar
1 small onion, finely chopped
2 bay leaves
1 tablespoon whole black peppercorns
1 tablespoon coriander seeds
3 cardamom seeds

Trim and discard mushroom stems. In a large saucepan bring remaining ingredients to the boil and simmer 10 minutes.

Strain liquid, return to saucepan and add mushrooms. Simmer 5 minutes, or until mushrooms are tender but not soft.

Pack mushrooms into sterilized jars. Pour pickling liquid to within ¼-inch of top. Seal with sterilized lids. Process for 20 minutes in a boiling-water bath for 1-pint containers. (Place jars on rack in processing pan. Do not allow jars to touch. Keep covered with 2-inches boiling water while processing.) Store in cool, dark place – allow to mellow 3 weeks before using.

Makes 4 pints.

PICCALILLI

½ large cauliflower
1 cucumber
½lb. tart green apples
6 tablespoons salt
1 quart water
1 lb. onions
2 fresh red chilies
3 cloves garlic
1½-in piece fresh gingerroot
½ cup vegetable oil
2 tablespoons each black peppercorns, turmeric and dry mustard
3 tablespoons cornstarch
4 quarts white wine vinegar

Chop cauliflower, peel and chop cucumber and apples. In a large, non-corosive bowl, mix salt and water. Add prepared vegetables. Cover and refrigerate overnight.

Chop onions, chilies, garlic and ginger. In a large skillet, fry onions in oil until soft. Add all ingredients, except last 2; cook 5 minutes.

Mix cornstarch and ½ cup vinegar. Pour remaining vinegar into skillet; stir in cornstarch/vinegar mixture. Cook, stirring until thickened. Drain vegetables soaking in brine. Wash under cold water. Add to sauce, simmer 10 minutes – vegetables should be crunchy. Pour into sterilized jars to within ½-inch of top. Seal with sterilized lids. Process, page 11. Store in cool, dark place – allow to mellow 2 to 5 months before using.

Makes about 6 pints.

MINT JELLY

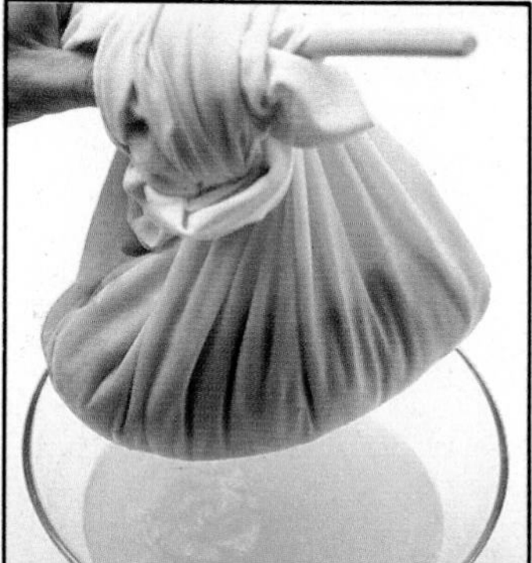

6 lb. tart green apples, quartered
Juice of 4 lemons
2 cups loosely packed fresh mint leaves
1 cup white wine vinegar
Sugar, see recipe
Chopped fresh mint leaves
Green food coloring
Mint extract, if desired

In a large heavy-bottomed saucepan, combine apples, lemon juice, mint; just cover with water. Simmer until apples are very soft. Add vinegar; simmer 5 minutes more.

Strain mixture through a jelly bag or double thickness of cheesecloth; do not force mixture through, as this will cloud jelly. Measure fruit juice and add 1 cup sugar for every cup of juice.

In a clean pan, cook juice and sugar over a low heat until sugar dissolves, stirring. Increase heat, boil briskly 5 minutes, without stirring, until temperature reaches 220F (105C). Or, test using spoon method, page 64. Stir in chopped mint, a little coloring and 1 to 2 teaspoons mint extract if desired. Pour jelly to within 1/8-inch of top into sterilized jars. Cover, seal tightly with sterilized lids. Invert jars for a few seconds to complete seal. Cool in upright position. Store in a cool, dark place.

Makes 6 to 8 pints.

Sage And Apple Jelly

6 lb. tart apples, washed, quartered (do not peel or core)
Juice of 4 lemons
1 cup white wine vinegar
Sugar, see recipe
1 cup loosely packed chopped sage, washed
6-8 sprigs of sage

In a preserving pan or a large, heavy-bottomed saucepan, combine apples and lemon juice; add enough water to cover fruit. Simmer until the apples are soft. Add vinegar and bring to boil, boil 5 minutes.

Strain mixture through a jelly bag or double thickness of cheesecloth for an hour. Do not press any apples through bag as this will cause jelly to cloud. Measure fruit mixture and add 1 cup of sugar for every cup of juice. Pour back into preserving pan, bring to boil, stirring until sugar dissolves. Boil until temperature reaches 220F (105C). Or test using spoon method, page 64. Stir in chopped sage.

Add sprigs of sage to sterilized jars. Pour jelly to within ⅛-inch of top of jars. Cover, seal tightly with sterilized lids. Invert jars for a few seconds to complete seal. Cool in upright position. Store in a cool, dark place.

Makes 6 to 8 pints.

PEACH CHUTNEY

2 lb. peaches, peeled, pitted and chopped
1 lb. onions, chopped
1¼ cups red wine vinegar
⅓ cup chopped, pitted dates
⅓ cup white raisins
1 teaspoon salt
½ teaspoon powdered ginger
½ teaspoon powdered cinnamon
¼ teaspoon powdered cloves
1 tablespoon mustard seeds
Grated peel and juice of 1 lemon
1½ cups packed brown sugar

In a large saucepan combine peaches with remaining ingredients, except sugar. Bring to a boil over high heat, stirring occasionally. Reduce heat and simmer peaches and onions until tender, stirring occasionally.

Add sugar and stir until dissolved. Simmer 2 to 3 hours, stirring frequently to prevent scorching, or until chutney is a rich brown color and thick.

Fill sterilized jars with chutney to within ¼-in of top. Seal with sterilized vinegar-proof lids. Process 15 minutes in boiling-water bath for 1-pint containers. (Place jars on a rack in processing pan. Do not allow jars to touch. Keep covered with 2-inches boiling water while processing.) Store in a cool, dark place – allow to mellow 6 weeks before using.

Makes about 3 pints.

SPICY APPLE CHUTNEY

2 lbs tart green apples
2 tablespoons salt
1 whole head garlic
1-inch piece fresh gingerroot
4 fresh green or red chilies, chopped (use red if you want a very hot chutney)
⅔ cup vegetable oil
2 tablespoons white mustard seeds
1 teaspoon fenugreek
15 whole black peppercorns
2 teaspoons powdered cumin
1 teaspoon chili powder
1 teaspoon turmeric
⅔ cup vinegar
½ cup sugar

Peel, core and slice apples. In a large glass or ceramic bowl, place apples; cover with salt; set aside. Peel and chop garlic and ginger, chop chilies.

In a large saucepan gently fry garlic and ginger in oil for 3 minutes. Add mustard seeds, fenugreek, peppercorns, cumin, chili powder, turmeric and fresh chilies to garlic and ginger. Cook 5 minutes longer.

Add apples, vinegar and sugar; simmer until chutney becomes thick. Fill sterilized jars with chutney to within ½-inch of top. Seal with sterilized vinegar-proof lids. Process 15 minutes in boiling-water bath for 1-pint jars. (Place jars on rack in processing pan. Do not allow jars to touch. Keep covered with 2 inches boiling water while processing.) Store in a cool, dark place.

Makes about 3 pints.

CHILI NUTS

2 cups unblanched whole almonds or peanuts
1 tablespoon chili powder
1 large clove garlic, crushed
¼ cup butter, chopped
Kosher salt

In a heavy skillet combine nuts, chili powder, garlic and butter.

Toss over medium heat until nuts become crisp and lightly browned.

Sprinkle with kosher salt and allow to cool. Store in airtight containers.

Makes about 2 cups.

SWEET SPICED NUTS

1 cup sugar
1 teaspoon salt
2 tablespoons powdered cinnamon
1 teaspoon powdered ginger
1 teaspoon powdered cloves
½ teaspoon powdered nutmeg
1 tablespoon water
1 egg white
1 cup whole nuts, such as peanuts, cashews or almonds

Preheat oven to 250F (120C). Using a coarse strainer sift sugar, salt and spices together 3 times. Beat together water and egg white. Dip nuts into egg white mixture.

Coat in sugar and spice mixture.

Spread nuts evenly on cookie sheet covered with baking parchment, making sure they don't touch. Bake 1½ to 2 hours. Remove from oven and allow to cool on cookie sheet. Shake excess sugar from nuts. Store in an airtight container.

Makes about 2 cups.

MEXICAN PEANUTS

20 small dried red or green chilies, according to taste, chopped
4 cloves garlic, crushed
2 tablespoons olive oil
2 lbs. blanched salted peanuts
1 teaspoon kosher salt
1 teaspoon chili powder

In a heavy skillet fry chilies and garlic in olive oil for a few minutes over low heat, stirring so chilies and garlic don't burn.

Add peanuts and continue frying and stirring until light brown.

Remove from heat and mix in kosher salt and chili powder. Cool. Store in airtight containers.

Makes about 2 lb.

MARINATED OLIVES

BLACK CARDAMOM OLIVES
1lb. large black olives in brine
1 orange
1 tablespoon cardamom seeds, crushed
Olive oil

Drain and rinse olives. Peel orange and cut skin (not white pith) into long strips. Place all ingredients into attractive jars and cover with olive oil.

GREEN CORIANDER OLIVES
1lb. large green olives in brine
8 to 10 cloves garlic
2 tablespoons coriander seeds, crushed
2 to 3 sprigs of fresh thyme
Olive oil

Drain and rinse olives. Place all ingredients into jars and cover with olive oil.

Cover and store Black Cardamom Olives and Green Coriander Olives in a cool, dark place. Allow to mellow at least 3 weeks before using.

Each recipe makes 1lb.

— Goat Cheese In Olive Oil —

½ lb. cylindrical goat cheese
4 large cloves garlic, peeled and sliced
3 or 4 sprigs of fresh rosemary and thyme
8 whole black peppercorns
Olive oil

Slice cheese into 8 equal rounds. Place in glass preserving jar with hinged lid.

Distribute garlic, herbs and peppercorns around cheese.

Cover with oil. Store in the refrigerator – allow to mellow 24 hours before using. Will keep up to 2 weeks.

Makes ½ lb.

SPIKED CHEESE BALLS

4 ounces blue cheese
4 ounces cream cheese
2 tablespoons vodka or Calvados (apple brandy)
2 tablespoons rye bread crumbs
¼ cup butter, softened
3 slices dark, rye bread, crusts removed
1 tablespoon caraway seeds
¼ cup almonds, toasted, finely ground

In a food processor or blender combine blue cheese, cream cheese and butter.

In a small bowl, mix vodka or Calvados with bread crumbs; let stand for 5 minutes. Blend bread crumbs with butter and cheese mixture; chill 30 minutes, or until firm enough to handle.

In a food processor or blender, blend rye bread and caraway seeds into fine crumbs. Roll about 2 teaspoons of cheese mixture into balls; roll half of the balls in rye bread mixture; half in almonds. Refrigerate until firm. Store in the refrigerator up to 1 week.

Each recipe makes about 30.

OLIVE CHEESE BALLS

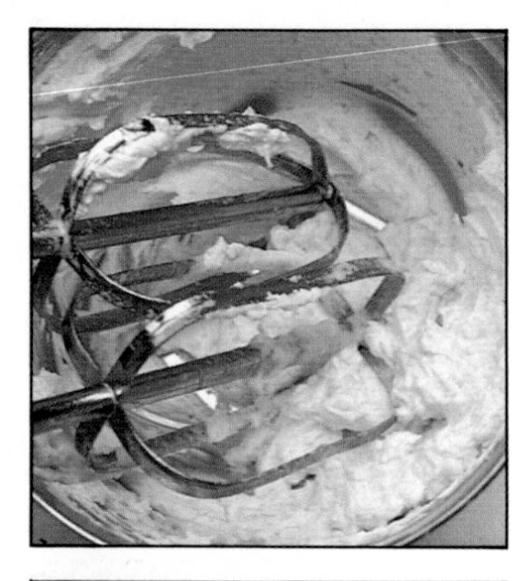

1 cup grated sharp Cheddar cheese, room temperature
3 tablespoons butter, softened
½ cup all-purpose flour
½ teaspoon cayenne pepper
25 to 30 medium-sized pitted or stuffed olives

Preheat oven to 400F (205C). In a bowl cream together cheese and butter. Sift flour with pepper.

Add flour mixture to creamed mixture. Knead mixture with hands until fairly smooth.

Cover each olive with a teaspoon of dough. Place on lightly greased cookie sheet. Bake 15 minutes, or until light golden brown. Cool on wire racks. Store in an airtight container in a cool place. Will keep up to 1 week.

Makes 25 to 30.

Cheese And Walnuts

½ cup butter, room temperature
12 ounces Cheddar cheese, grated
6 tablespoons beer
½ teaspoon Dijon mustard
1 teaspoon Worcestershire sauce
½ teaspoon white pepper
⅔ cup walnut halves

In a bowl beat butter until light and fluffy.

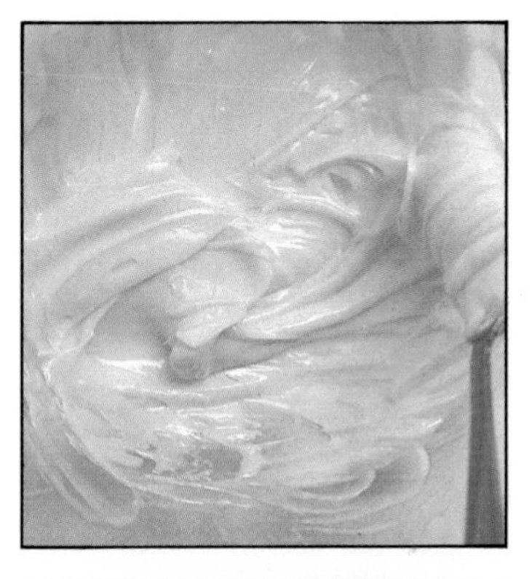

Add cheese and beer alternately, beating until well combined. Stir in remaining ingredients, except walnuts. Line a small container or ramekin with plastic wrap.

Place half walnuts on bottom of container. Spoon half the cheese over walnuts. Cover with remaining walnuts; then remaining cheese. Smooth top. Refrigerate 24 hours. Turn out, upside down, onto serving plate. Cover. Store in the refrigerator. Will keep up to 10 days.

Makes about 1½ lbs.

— STUFFED CHERRY TOMATOES —

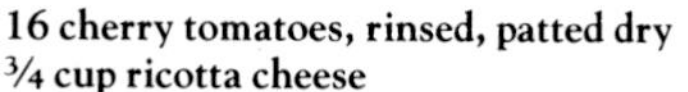

16 cherry tomatoes, rinsed, patted dry
¾ cup ricotta cheese
8 fresh basil leaves, minced
3 ounces soft blue cheese
¼ cup cottage cheese, sieved
2 tablespoons fresh chopped chives
Ground black pepper
Celery leaves and chive sprigs for decoration

With a sharp knife, cut cap off tomatoes. With a small spoon remove seeds and turn tomatoes upside down onto paper towels to drain.

Beat ricotta cheese until smooth. Stir in basil and add pepper. Blend blue cheese with cottage cheese and chives until smooth. Add pepper.

With a small spoon, pack half the tomatoes with ricotta mixture and half with blue cheese mixture. Cover with caps, garnish with celery leaves and chive sprigs. Chill.

Makes 12 to 16.

PEARS STUFFED WITH GORGONZOLA

8 small ripe pears, peeled
Juice of 3 lemons, in a large bowl
1/4 lb. Gorgonzola cheese, softened
1/4 cup butter, softened
1/4 cup, finely chopped walnuts or pistachio nuts

Slice pears in half, taking care to leave stem intact on one half. Core pears; using a spoon, remove a tablespoon of the flesh to form a hollow. Immediately immerse pears in bowl with lemon juice to prevent discoloration.

In a small bowl, beat together cheese and butter until smooth. Fill each pear half with about a tablespoon of mixture.

Press pears together and roll in walnuts. Refrigerate at least 2 hours. Serve as first course. Store in the refrigerator up to 3 days.

Makes 8 servings.

BRIDGE CANAPÉS

Slices of white and brown bread, crusts removed
Cream cheese, softened
Red and black caviar
Thin slices of salami
Black olives, sliced or whole
Hard-cooked eggs, sliced
Thin slices ham
Thin strips of red pepper, for decoration

Preheat oven to 200F (100C). Using cookie cutters in shapes such as spades, hearts, diamonds and clubs, cut shapes from bread and bake until dry. Cool on a wire rack.

Cover canapés with cream cheese.

Decorate with red and black caviar, thin slices of salami, black olives, hard-cooked eggs, thin slices of ham and strips of red pepper. Use different garnishes for each shape of canapé.

FRITTATA

2 tablespoons olive oil
4 large onions, thinly sliced
2 cloves garlic, minced
3 cups sliced zucchini
1 red chili, minced, if desired
Salt and pepper
8 eggs

In a large non-stick skillet heat oil. Fry onions until soft. Add garlic and cook one minute more. Add zucchini and cook until just soft. Stir in chili, if desired.

Beat eggs with salt and pepper. Pour over vegetables; stir gently.

Cook mixture until base is firm but eggs are still somewhat soft. Place pan under hot broiler and brown top. Turn onto a platter and serve warm or cold. Store in the refrigerator up to 3 days.

Makes 1 frittata.

BLUE CHEESE DIP AND CRACKERS

BLUE CHEESE DIP

1½ cups blue cheese, chopped
1 cup drained crushed pineapple
½ cup sour cream
½ cup cottage cheese
2 tablespoons fresh chopped chives
Chive sprigs, finely chopped chives, radish slices for decoration

In a food processor or blender, blend all ingredients, except chive sprigs.

When just combined, pour into bowl or bowls.

Cover. Store in the refrigerator up to 1 week. Decorate with chive sprigs, finely chopped chives and radish slices.

Makes about 2½ cups.

CHEDDAR CHEESE CRACKERS

⅔ cup wholewheat flour
2 tablespoons self-raising flour
½ teaspoon salt
¼ teaspoon cayenne pepper
½ cup butter
½ cup grated Cheddar cheese
1 tablespoon lemon juice
1 egg

Preheat oven 325F (160C). In food processor or blender, combine all ingredients. Blend until dough is formed. Shape mixture into a roll 15 inches long. Wrap in plastic wrap. Refrigerate at least 3 hours. Cut roll into slices ¼-in thick, place on lightly greased cookie sheets. Bake 15 minutes. Cool.
Makes about 60.

BRAN CRACKERS

½ cup unprocessed bran
¾ cup wholewheat flour
1 tablespoon packed brown sugar
½ cup butter
2 eggs
Pinch of salt

Preheat oven to 325F (160C). In a food processor or blender, combine bran, wholewheat flour, sugar and butter. Blend until butter is completely cut into flour mixture. Add eggs and salt. Blend until dough forms. Turn mixture out onto a floured board and knead lightly. Divide dough in half. Press each half into greased 11 x 7-in baking pan. Prick surface with fork. Bake 15 minutes. Cut into squares. Cool.
Makes about 35.

PEARL BALLS WITH DIPPING SAUCE

1 1/4 cups white long grain rice
4 dried Chinese mushrooms, or 6 fresh shiitake mushrooms
1/2 lb. ground veal
1/2 lb. ground pork
4 green onions, finely chopped
5 water chestnuts, sliced
1 teaspoon fresh grated gingerroot
1 clove garlic, crushed
2 tablespoons soy sauce
1 egg, beaten
1 teaspoon salt

DIPPING SAUCE:

1/2 cup soy sauce
1/2 teaspoon sesame oil
1 tablespoon chili sauce

Soak rice in cold water 2 hours. Drain and spread onto kitchen towels. Soak dried Chinese mushrooms in hot water for 30 minutes, squeeze out water and finely chop. If using fresh mushrooms do not soak. In a large bowl combine mushrooms and remaining ingredients. Mix well.

Roll mixture into walnut-sized balls. Roll in rice to coat completely. Place in steamer. Steam over boiling water 30 minutes, or until rice has swollen and is completely cooked.

DIPPING SAUCE:

In a small bowl, combine all ingredients.

Makes about 30.

CHINESE CHICKEN WINGS

2 lb. chicken wings
2 tablespoons peanut oil
2 teaspoons sesame oil
½ cup soy sauce
2 tablespoons honey
2 cloves garlic, crushed
1 teaspoon freshly grated gingerroot
½ teaspoon five spice powder
2 tablespoons dry sherry, if desired

Cut tips off chicken wings and discard. Place wings in a large bowl.

In a bowl, mix remaining ingredients. Pour over chicken wings; stir to coat wings well. Cover; refrigerate 4 hours or overnight.

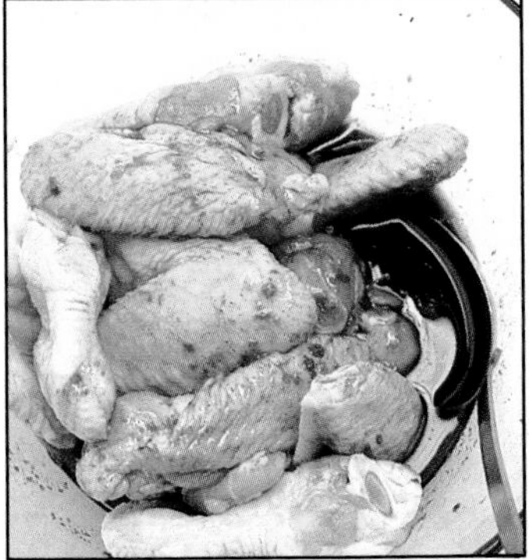

Preheat oven to 350F (180C). Place wings on lightly greased cookie sheet. Bake wings 30 minutes; turn and continue baking until they are golden brown, about 10 minutes. Drain on paper towels. Store in the refrigerator up to 3 days.

Makes about 24.

SEAFOOD DIP

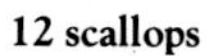

12 scallops
1 package (8 oz) cream cheese, cut into chunks
¼ cup Mayonnaise, page 10
3 green onions, chopped (use white part only)
1 small pickle, finely chopped
2 teaspoons finely chopped fresh coriander (cilantro) or parsley
½ teaspoon chili sauce
Salt and pepper
20 shrimp, shelled, deveined, cooked

Poach scallops until they are just opaque, being careful not to overcook. In a food processor or blender, place cream cheese, Mayonnaise, 6 scallops, green onion, pickle, coriander and chili sauce; blend. Add salt and pepper and adjust other seasonings if necessary.

Chop remaining scallops and all but a few shrimp. Combine with cream cheese mixture.

Spoon into decorative serving containers. Decorate with remaining shrimp. Store in the refrigerator up to 2 days.

Makes about 2½ cups.

Potted Salmon

½ lb. smoked salmon
1 cup clarified butter
½ teaspoon ground white pepper
Pinch of salt
Fresh chives, to decorate

Blend or process salmon, ¾ cup clarified butter and pepper.

Blend or process to a fine paste. Add salt to taste and refrigerate until firm. Press into small attractive dishes.

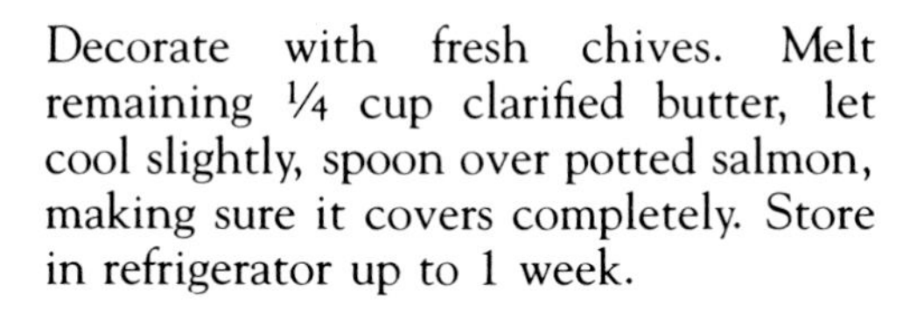

Decorate with fresh chives. Melt remaining ¼ cup clarified butter, let cool slightly, spoon over potted salmon, making sure it covers completely. Store in refrigerator up to 1 week.

Makes about 16.

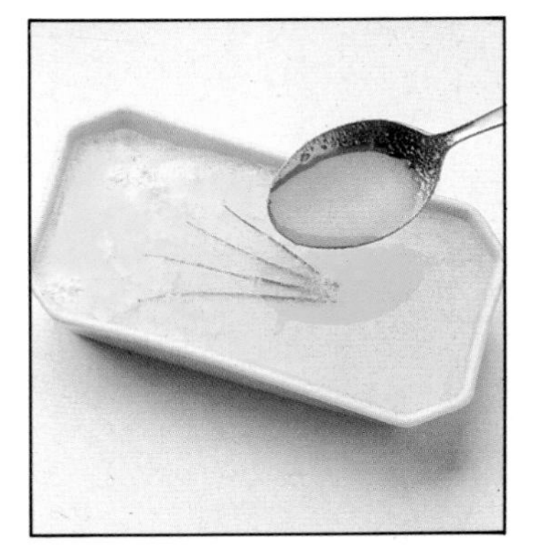

FISH PÂTÉ

1 quart water
1/4 cup dry vermouth
1 small carrot, chopped
1 small onion, chopped
1 stalk celery, chopped
1 teaspoon black peppercorns
1 teaspoon salt
Sprig of parsley
Small piece of fresh fennel and thyme
1 bay leaf
1/2 lb. fish fillets
2 teaspoons gelatin
2 tablespoons pimiento, chopped
1 green onion, finely chopped
Salt and pepper
Radishes, cucumber, lemon slices, and red and black caviar, to garnish.

In a saucepan combine first 10 ingredients. Bring to boil; reduce heat and simmer 30 minutes. Add fish; poach 10 minutes until flesh flakes when tested with a fork.

Remove fillets; cool and flake; discarding any bones and set aside. Reduce stock to 1½ cups. Cool. When just warm, sprinkle gelatin on surface, stir to dissolve. Place fish, pimiento, green onion, salt and pepper in a food processor, purée to desired texture, gradually adding fish stock.

Pour into a 3-cup mold, refrigerate until set. To unmold, place container briefly into hot water and turn out onto a platter. Refrigerate. Serve garnished. Store in the refrigerator up to 3 days.

Makes about 2 lb.

Chicken Liver Pâté

1 cup finely chopped onions
1 cup unsalted butter
2 cloves garlic, finely chopped
1½ lb. chicken livers, cleaned, fibrous membrane removed
2 hard-cooked eggs
2 tablespoons brandy
¼ teaspoon powdered cloves
½ teaspoon powdered allspice
½ teaspoon white pepper
½ teaspoon salt

In a large, heavy-bottomed skillet, gently cook onions in butter until soft. Add garlic and chicken livers and cook until the livers are nicely browned on outside, but still pink on inside.

In a food processor or blender, combine contents of skillet with remaining ingredients. Blend until the desired texture is achieved. It may be necessary to do this in batches.

Pack into ungreased 9 x 5-inch loaf pan, terrine or pâté mold. Press firmly to make sure mixture fills corners. Cover tightly and refrigerate. Top may be weighted with brick if firmer pâté is desired. Store, well wrapped, in refrigerator up to 7 days.

Makes about 2¼ lb.

GRAND MARNIER PÂTÉ

1½ lb. pork livers, cleaned, fibrous membrane removed
½ lb. bacon, cut into pieces
½ cup butter, melted
1 medium-size onion, chopped
¼ cup Grand Marnier (or other orange liqueur)
2 teaspoons grated orange peel
2 tablespoons all-purpose flour
2 eggs, beaten
2 teaspoons salt
1 teaspoon white pepper
½ teaspoon powdered cloves
½ teaspoon powdered allspice
½ teaspoon powdered sage
¼ teaspoon each powdered mace and powdered nutmeg
3 tablespoons whipping cream

Preheat oven to 350F (180C). In a food processor or blender, mix livers, bacon, butter and onion until a smooth purée; add liqueur and orange peel. It may be necessary to do this in batches.

In a bowl, mix together flour, eggs, salt, pepper, cloves, allspice, sage, mace, nutmeg, cream and pureed liver.

Pack into an ungreased 9 x 5-in loaf pan, temire on pâté mold. Put pan into a larger, deep baking dish. Fill larger baking dish with hot water to level of pâté mixture. Bake for 2½ to 3 hours in baking pan. Cool. Remove pâté from larger baking dish and cool in baking pan.

Orange Glaze:

1 ½ cups clear chicken stock
1 ½ teaspoons gelatine
2 tablespoons Grand Marnier (or other orange liqueur)
Thin slices of orange, small sprigs of rosemary, celery leaves, black olives and strips of red pepper, for decoration

Orange Glaze:

Warm chicken stock, sprinkle gelatin over surface and stir to dissolve slightly and add Grand Marnier. Decorate pâté with orange slices, small sprigs of rosemary, celery leaves, black olives and strips of red pepper.

Gently spoon the gelatine mixture over pâté a little at a time.

Store in the refrigerator; allow to set 24 hours before using. Will keep up to 1 week well-wrapped.

Makes about 3 lb.

PORK AND VEAL TERRINE

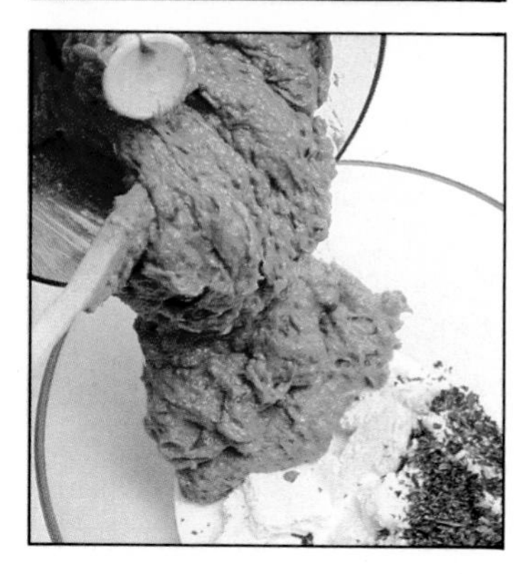

2 onions, finely chopped
2 cloves garlic, crushed
½ cup unsalted butter, chopped
½ lb. each ground pork and veal
½ lb. chicken livers, cleaned, fibrous membrane removed
½ lb. pork livers, cleaned, fibrous membrane removed
1 cup good quality white bread pieces, crusts removed
½ cup milk
¼ cup dry vermouth
1 teaspoon dried thyme
½ teaspoon dried marjoram
½ teaspoon dried oregano
½ teaspoon dried sage
1 teaspoon salt
½ teaspoon black pepper
8 strips bacon
3 to 4 bay leaves

Preheat oven to 350F (175C). In a skillet, fry onions and garlic in butter over low heat until soft.

In food processor or blender, purée together cooked onions and garlic with ground pork and veal, and chicken and pork livers until smooth. It may be necessary to do this in batches.

In a large bowl, soak bread with milk and vermouth until soft. Add puréed mixture to bread and milk mixture. Stir in herbs and salt and pepper. Mix thoroughly.

Line a 9 x 5-in loaf pan, terrine pan or pâté mold with bacon allowing strips to hang over sides. Strips should be placed parallel to one another and crosswise in pan. Fill pan with meat mixture, pressing it into sides and corners.

Cover top with a line of bay leaves and fold the bacon over top of mixture. Cover tightly with foil (and lid if using terrine pan). Put into a larger, deep baking dish. Fill larger baking dish with hot water to level of meat mixture. Bake 2½ to 3 hours. Remove terrine from larger baking dish and place a weight (such as a brick) over the foil, pressing down on meat mixture.

Store in the refrigerator 12 hours. Remove weight. A further 12 hours or longer in the refrigerator will give the terrine a better flavor. Serve with Melba toast, or French bread. Store in refrigerator up to 1 week.

Makes about 3½ lb.

RILLETTES

3 lb.pork belly
1 pigs foot, chopped in half
1 lb.pork neck
1 lb.back fat
2 cloves garlic, chopped
2 sprigs fresh thyme
1 bay leaf
¼ teaspoon each powdered cloves, nutmeg, ginger
½ teaspoon powdered cinnamon
1 tablespoon salt
1 tablespoon white pepper
1 cup white wine

Preheat oven to 300F (150C). Cube pork and fat into even-sized pieces. In a large heavy casserole combine pork, fat and remaining ingredients. Cover with foil; bake 5 hours. Strain over a bowl. Set liquid aside.

Remove meat from bones; using two forks shred meat. Adjust for seasoning and add a little of reserved liquid so texture is slightly creamy.

Pack meat firmly into pâté mold, terrine or 9 x 5-inch loaf pan. Carefully pour melted fat, which has been separated from reserved liquid, onto meat to a depth of ½-inch. Cover. Store in the refrigerator – allow to mellow 3 days before serving. Will keep up to 2 weeks.

Makes about 5 lb.

Spanakopita

1 lb. fresh spinach, washed, and stems removed
½ lb. feta cheese
2 tablespoons finely chopped shallots
2 onions, thinly sliced
1 tablespoon finely chopped thyme
1 tablespoon finely chopped rosemary
2 tablespoons finely chopped oregano
2 tablespoons finely chopped fennel
6 eggs
½ cup vegetable oil
1 teaspoon salt
Fresh ground pepper
14 sheets filo pastry
¾ cup butter, melted

Preheat oven to 350F (175C). Steam spinach leaves until limp. Cool; squeeze out all moisture. Combine spinach with cheese, shallots, onion and herbs. Set aside. In separate bowl, beat together eggs, oil, salt and pepper. Stir egg mixture into spinach mixture.

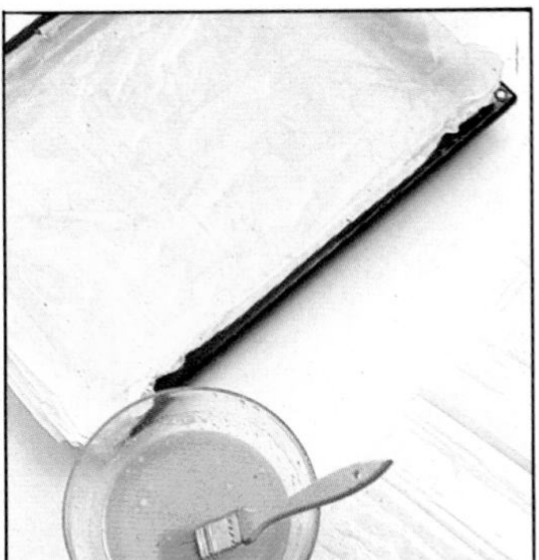

Brush a 13 x 9-in baking pan with a little of the melted butter. Lay a sheet of filo on pan and brush lightly with butter. Repeat using 6 more sheets.

Pour filling over filo layers. Top with remaining filo sheets, brushing each layer with melted butter. Trim and tuck edges to neaten. Bake 45 minutes, or until pie is golden brown. Cut into squares. Serve warm or cold. Store in the refrigerator up to 3 days.

Makes 1 pie.

English Pork Pies

Stock:

3½ cups water
2 pigs feet
1 large marrow bone
2 onions, chopped
Fresh bouquet garni
Pinch of salt
1 teaspoon ground white pepper

In a large saucepan, bring all ingredients to a boil. Lower heat, simmer 3 hours and allow to reduce to about 2½ cups. Strain, cool, skim off fat. Set stock aside.

Pastry:

½ lb. shortening, chopped
2 cups all-purpose plain flour
Pinch of salt
2 teaspoons baking soda
boiling water

In a bowl, combine flour, salt and baking soda. Cut in shortening until mixture resembles coarse meal. Add sufficient boiling water to flour mixture to form into a stiff dough. Cover; leave to rest.

Preheat oven to 400F (205C). On a floured board, roll pastry to ⅛-in thick. Cut eight 6-in circles and eight 3-in circles. Press 6-in circles into greased patty tins.

Filling:
2 lb. lean pork, diced
1 teaspoon salt
½ teaspoon ground white pepper
¼ teaspoon each of ground mace, ground nutmeg and ground coriander
½ teaspoon ground thyme
2 fresh sage leaves, chopped
1 egg, beaten

In a bowl, combine pork, salt, pepper, spices and herbs. Mix thoroughly and fill pastry-lined patty tins to within ¼-in of top. Brush edges of pastry with water. Top with 3-in circles; crimp edges to seal. Cut steam vents in tops. Brush tops with beaten egg.

Bake pies 20 minutes; lower oven temperature to 300F (150C) and bake 45 minutes. If pastry becomes too dark, cover loosely with foil. Remove pies from oven. Using a funnel pour 2 to 3 tablespoons of prepared stock into each pie through hole in top.

Allow to cool; remove from patty tins. Store, covered, in cool place – allow to mellow 12 hours. Will keep up to 3 days.

Makes about 8 pies.

LEMON CURD

1 cup sugar
¼ cup butter, chopped
grated peel of 2 lemons
juice of 3 lemons
3 eggs, beaten

In a heatproof bowl or top of double boiler placed over a saucepan of hot water, combine sugar, butter, lemon peel and lemon juice.

Place over low heat, cook until butter melts, stirring occasionally.

Stir in eggs (do not let mixture boil, or it will curdle). Continue stirring over heat until mixture thickens. Pour into sterilized jars, seal, cool. Store in the refrigerator. Will keep up to 2 weeks. Use as a filling for tart shells or as a spread on muffins.

Makes 1 pint.

— Honey And Apricot Spread —

12 dried apricots
1 cup creamed honey

In a bowl, place apricots, cover with boiling water; allow to stand at room temperature until softened.

Drain apricots. In blender or food processor, process apricots and honey.

When thoroughly combined, pour into a sterilized jar, seal with a sterilized lid; cool. Store in the refrigerator – allow to mellow 24 hours before using. You can easily double or triple this recipe.

Makes about 2 cups.

APRICOT AND ALMOND CONSERVE

1 lb. dried apricots, quartered
5 cups water
6 cups sugar
½ teaspoon almond liqueur or almond extract
½ cup blanched, slivered almonds

Soak apricots overnight in water. Strain apricots; reserve liquid.

In a heavy-bottomed saucepan combine reserved liquid and sugar; bring to boil over a low heat stirring until sugar is dissolved. Add apricots and simmer until proper consistency is reached and candy thermometer reaches 220F (105C). Or test using spoon method described in Grapefruit Marmalade page 64.

Immediately stir in liqueur and almonds. Remove from heat. Allow jam to stand at room temperature 10 minutes, stirring occasionally, to keep fruit and nuts in suspension. Pour conserve to within ⅛-inch of top of sterilized jars. Seal tightly with sterilized lids. Invert jars for a few seconds to complete seal. Cool in upright position. Store in a cool, dark place.

Makes 4 pints.

MINCEMEAT

1 1/4 cups raisins
1 1/4 cups currants
1/2 cup mixed candied peel
2 tart green apples, peeled
grated peel of 1 lemon
grated peel of 1 orange
3/4 cup packed brown sugar
1/2 cup butter, melted
1/2 teaspoon each of powdered nutmeg and powdered cinnamon
1/4 teaspoon ground cloves
2/3 cup brandy

Finely chop the raisins, currants and mixed peel, place in a bowl.

Chop apples and add with lemon and orange peel, brown sugar, melted butter, spices and brandy to raisin mixture. Combine well. Cover and set aside in a cool place for 3 days. Stir twice a day.

Spoon into sterilized jars, seal. Store in the refrigerator – allow to mellow 2 weeks before using.

Makes about 6 cups.

GRAPEFRUIT MARMALADE

4 lb. grapefruit, well scrubbed
6 to 9 cups sugar

Cut grapefruit into quarters, remove seeds and pithy centers. Put the seeds and centers in a 6-inch square of cheesecloth, tie into a bag. Peel grapefruit. Cut peel into julienne strips. Slice peeled fruit crosswise into thin slices. Separate slices into individual sections. Place fruit and bag in a large bowl; just cover with water. Soak 12 hours. Remove bag. In large preserving pan or saucepan, simmer fruit and soaking water 1 hour. For every cup of fruit and water add 3/4 cup sugar. Bring to a boil; boil about 20 minutes or to proper consistency.

Test marmalade for doneness immediately after boiling. Proper consistency is reached when candy thermometer reaches 220F (105C). Or, test by spoon test. Pour a small amount of marmalade onto a cold plate. Let stand until cold. If marmalade forms a skin and wrinkles when pushed with a finger or spoon, it is ready. Remove pan from heat while test preserve is cooling.

Cool 10 minutes; stir gently to mix skin through the marmalade. Pour into sterilized jars to within 1/2-inch of top. Seal with sterilized lids. Invert jars for a few seconds. Cool in upright position. Store in cool, dark place.

Makes about 5 pints.

Rum And Plum Jam

2 lb. plums
2 lemons
5¾ cups sugar
2 tablespoons dark rum

Pit and finely chop the plums; squeeze juice from lemons. In a large heavy-bottomed saucepan combine fruit, sugar and lemon juice.

Bring to a boil over a low heat, stirring until sugar is dissolved. Increase the heat and boil 10 minutes, stirring to avoid burning. Begin testing for proper consistency. Proper consistency is reached when candy thermometer reaches 220F (105C).

Or, test using spoon method described in Grapefruit Marmalade, page 64. Remove pan from heat and stir in rum. Allow jam to stand 10 minutes, stirring at intervals so fruit doesn't sink. Pour to within ⅛-inch of top of sterilized jars. Seal tightly with sterilized lids. Invert jars for a few seconds to complete seal. Cool in upright position. Store in a cool, dark place.

Makes about 4 pints.

MIXED CURRANT JELLY

2 lb.red currants, washed
2 lb.black currants, washed
6 cups water
Sugar, see recipe

In a preserving pan combine fruit and water. Bring to boil and simmer until very soft.

Mash fruit with a wooden spoon and spoon into a jelly bag to drip overnight. Measure fruit juice and allow 1 cup sugar for each cup of juice.

Place sugar and liquid back in pan and bring to boil, stirring to dissolve sugar. Boil 7 minutes. Begin testing for proper consistency. Proper consistency is reached when candy thermometer reaches 220F (105C). Or test using spoon method described in Grapefruit Marmalade page 64. Pour into sterilized jars. Seal tightly with sterilized lids. Invert jars for a few seconds to complete seal. Cool in upright position. Store in a cool, dark place.

Makes about 8 pints.

— MICROWAVE STRAWBERRY JAM —

1 lb. strawberries, washed, hulled, sliced
Juice of 1 lemon
1 1/3 cups sugar
1 tablespoon butter

In a large bowl combine strawberries, lemon juice and sugar. Cook 20 minutes on high power, stirring occasionally.

Check for proper consistency by measuring temperature of jam with a candy thermometer. Jam is done when 220F (105C). Or, test by spoon method described in Grapefruit Marmalade page 64.

Stir butter into jam until dissolved. Allow jam to stand 30 minutes before bottling. Pour jam to within 1/8-in of top of sterilized jars. Seal tightly with sterilized lids. Invert jars for a few seconds to complete seal. Cool in upright position. Store in a cool, dark place.

Makes about 2 pints.

— ROSEMARY AND QUINCE JELLY —

6 lb. quinces
Juice of 3 lemons
Sugar, see recipe
3 tablespoons finely chopped rosemary
6-8 sprigs of rosemary

Wash and coarsely chop quinces, combine quinces and lemon juice in preserving pan or large, heavy-bottomed saucepan. Cover with water. Simmer uncovered until quinces are very soft. Strain mixture through a jelly bag or double thickness of cheesecloth, being careful not to force mixture through, as this will cloud jelly.

Measure fruit juice and add 1 cup of sugar for every cup of juice. Return to pan, bring to a rolling boil. Boil briskly for 5 minutes until temperature reaches 220F (105C). Or test using spoon method, page 64.

Add finely chopped rosemary. Add sprigs of rosemary to sterilized jars. Pour jelly to within ⅛-inch of jars. Cover, seal tightly with sterilized lids. Invert jars for a few seconds to complete seal. Cool in upright position. Store in a cool, dark place.

Makes 6 to 8 pints.

FIGS IN BRANDY

14 dried whole figs
½ cup sugar
1 cinnamon stick
Approximately 1 cup brandy

In a large saucepan or skillet, place figs in one layer with sugar and cinnamon stick. Just cover with water. Poach over low heat for 5 minutes. Discard cinnamon stick. Drain figs, reserve syrup.

Pack figs in sterilized jar. Reduce syrup to half by simmering uncovered.

Half fill jar of figs with brandy. Pour reduced syrup in jar to within ½-inch of top, cover. Store in a cool dark place – allow to mellow at least 1 month before using.

Makes 1½ pints.

Brandied Peaches

2 cups sugar
1 cup water
2 lb. peaches, halved, pitted and skinned (treat with lemon juice to prevent discoloration, if desired)
Pinch of ground nutmeg
Approximately 1 cup brandy

Combine sugar and water in large saucepan. Heat to dissolve sugar. Add fruit and nutmeg to syrup and simmer until the fruit is just tender. Drain fruit (reserve syrup) and pack into sterilized jars.

Bring reserved syrup to a rolling boil. Boil, until reduced by half.

Half fill jars with brandy. Pour syrup into jars to within ½-inch of top. If syrup runs short fill jars with more brandy. Seal. Store in a cool, dark place – allow to mellow 1 month before using.

Makes 2 pints.

PRUNES IN RUM

1 lb. prunes
½ cup sugar
1 cup water
Cinnamon stick
Peel of 1 lemon, cut into strips
Approximately 1 cup dark rum

In a saucepan gently combine prunes, sugar, water, cinnamon stick and lemon peel. Poach 5 minutes. Lift out prunes using slotted spoon. Slit prunes lengthwise; pit. Pack prunes into a sterilized jar.

Boil syrup until reduced to ⅓ of a cup. Remove peel and cinnamon stick. Cool. Half fill jar with rum.

Top with syrup, adding more rum to cover prunes if necessary. Cover tightly. Store in a cool place – allow to mellow for 3 weeks. Will keep up to 3 months.

Makes about 1½ pints.

MACEDOINE OF FRUIT IN BRANDY

1lb. mixed berries such as strawberries, raspberries, blueberries and gooseberries; rinsed
2lb. sugar
Approximately 2 cups brandy
1lb. mixed peeled, pitted peaches, plums, nectarines and apricots; halved

In a sterilized preserving jar, layer berries with sugar.

Pour brandy over to cover.

Layer peach, plum, nectarine and apricot halves with remaining sugar over berries. Pour brandy over to cover. Continue layering to ½-inch from top of jar. Seal. Process 30 minutes in boiling-water bath for 1-pint containers (place jars on rack in processing pan. Do not allow jars to touch. Keep covered with 2 inches boiling water while processing.) Store in a cool, dark place – allow to mellow at least 2 months before using.

RUM BUTTER

2 egg yolks
1 tablespoon sugar
2 tablespoons rum
½ teaspoon vanilla extract
½ cup butter, softened
Iced water

Combine yolks and sugar in a heatproof bowl or in top of a double boiler placed over a saucepan of hot water. Beat yolks until they thicken and turn pale. Add rum and vanilla. Beat to combine.

Place a bowl or top of double boiler into large bowl of iced water. Beat egg mixture 1 minute to cool slightly. Beat in butter, a tablespoon at a time, until mixture is well combined.

Spoon into a container to firm. The mixture may be piped onto a plate when slightly softened if desired. Store the rosettes in one layer, covered, in the refrigerator. Will keep up to 1 week.

Makes about ¾ cup.

— OLD FASHIONED GINGER BEER —

2 lemons
3 cups sugar
1 oz piece fresh gingerroot, peeled and bruised
2 teaspoons cream of tartar
1½ tablespoons brewers yeast
5 quarts boiling water

Carefully remove peel from lemons; remove and discard all white pith. Slice lemons thinly, removing seeds.

In a large glass or earthenware bowl, place lemon slices, peel, sugar, ginger and cream of tartar. Pour boiling water over mixture; let stand until tepid. Add brewers yeast and let stand in a warm place for at least 24 hours, or up to 2 days.

Skim the yeast from the top and strain liquid through cheesecloth into sterilized bottles. Seal. Store in the refrigerator – allow to mellow 3 days before using.

Makes 5 quarts.

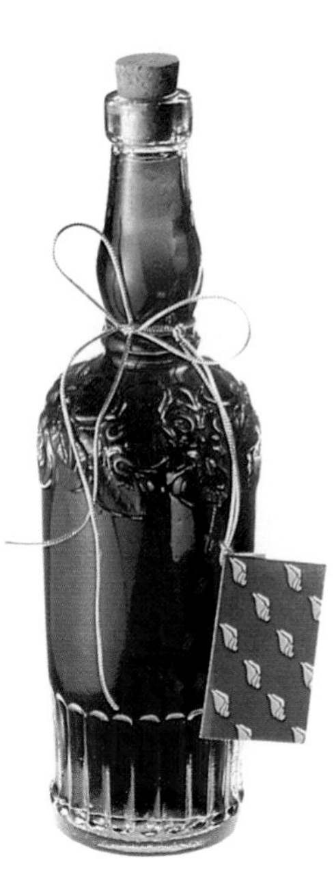

Coffee Liqueur

2 cups water
$4\frac{1}{2}$ cups sugar
4 teaspoons instant coffee powder
Few drops vanilla extract
1 cup brandy
1 cup rum

In a saucepan combine water, sugar, instant coffee and vanilla. Heat gently, stirring until sugar and coffee have dissolved. Cool.

Stir brandy and rum into syrup.

Into a large decanter, pour coffee liqueur. Seal. Store in a cool, dark place – allow to mellow 2 to 3 weeks before using.

Makes about 2 quarts.

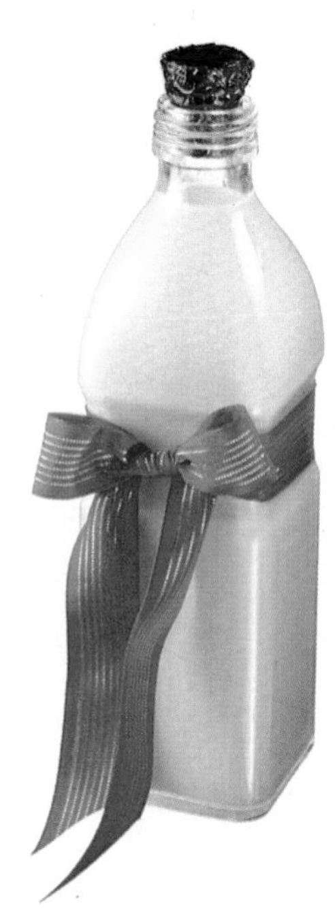

IRISH CREAM WHISKEY

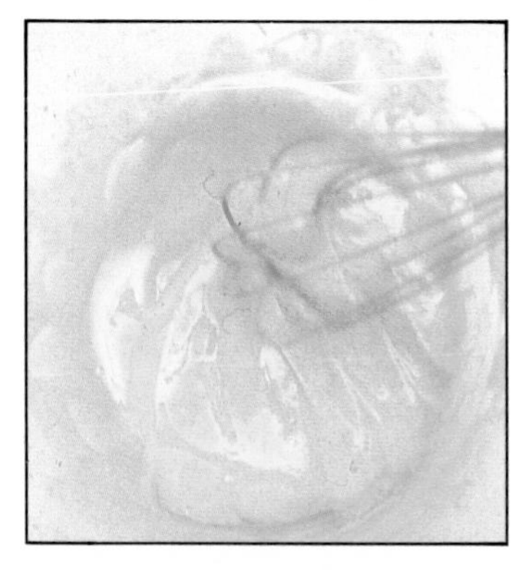

3 egg yolks
1 (14 oz.) can sweetened condensed milk
1¼ cups whipping cream
1½ cups whiskey
1½ tablespoons sweetened chocolate syrup
¼ teaspoon coconut extract

In a large bowl, beat egg yolks until thick.

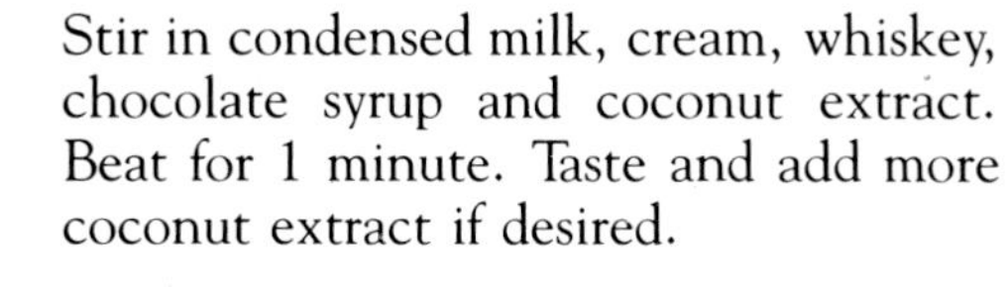

Stir in condensed milk, cream, whiskey, chocolate syrup and coconut extract. Beat for 1 minute. Taste and add more coconut extract if desired.

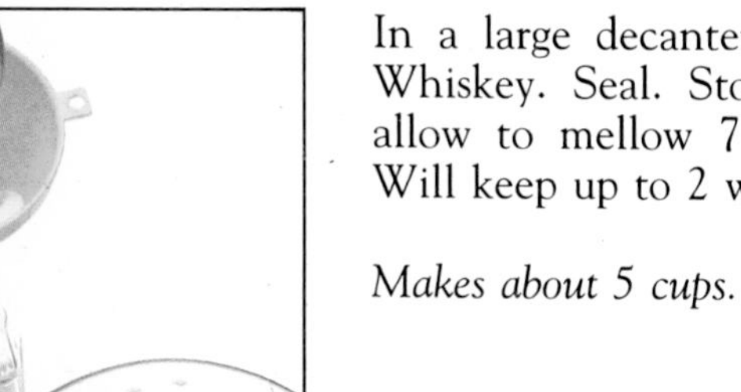

In a large decanter pour Irish Cream Whiskey. Seal. Store in refrigerator – allow to mellow 7 days before using. Will keep up to 2 weeks.

Makes about 5 cups.

Peppermint Liqueur

1 cup water
2 cups sugar
1 teaspoon peppermint extract
1½ cups brandy
Approximately ½ teaspoon green food coloring

In a saucepan, combine water and sugar gently stirring. Heat until sugar dissolves. Cool.

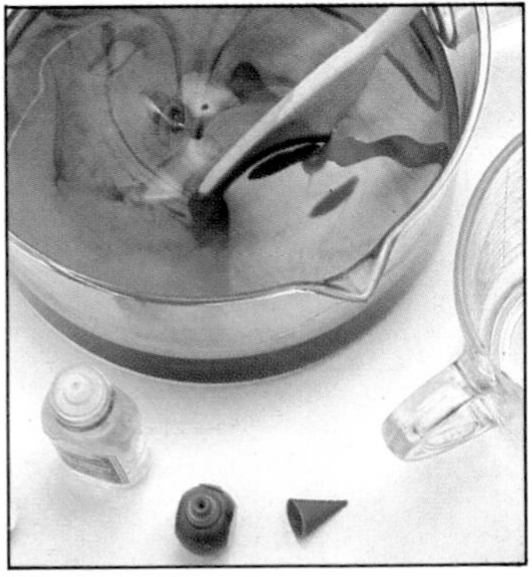

Stir in peppermint extract, brandy and enough food coloring to make the syrup the color of crème de menthe. Pour into a sterilized decanter or bottle.

Seal and shake. Store in a cool dark place – allow to mellow 7 days before using.

Makes about 1 quart.

BLUEBERRY OR BLACKBERRY JELLIES

2 lb. fresh blueberries or blackberries, washed
2 cups sugar
2 tablespoons unsalted butter
1½ cups liquid pectin
Superfine sugar

Line a 10-inch square pan with wax or baking parchment. In a food processor or blender, place fruit and 1 cup sugar. Purée. It may be necessary to do this in batches. Pass fruit through a food mill, or force through a fine strainer into a large saucepan containing remaining 1 cup sugar.

Stirring constantly, bring fruit to boil and continue stirring and boiling 2 minutes more. Add butter and continue stirring and boiling 2 minutes more. Remove saucepan from heat. Add pectin, stirring until well combined. Pour into prepared pan and allow to set in cool place overnight.

Cut jelly into attractive shapes and roll in sugar. Store in a cool place in airtight containers with wax paper separating the layers. Will keep for up to 1 week.

Makes about 2 lb.

KIWI FRUIT JELLIES

2 lb. kiwi fruit, peeled and chopped
Juice of 1 lemon
3 cups sugar
2 tablespoons unsalted butter
1 cup liquid pectin
Green food coloring, if desired
Superfine sugar

Line an 8 x 10-inch pan with wax or parchment paper. In a food processor or blender, combine fruit, lemon juice and 1 cup sugar.

Purée. It may be necessary to do this in batches. Pass the liquid through a food mill or fine strainer into a large saucepan. Add remaining sugar; stirring constantly, bring to boil. Boil for 3 minutes; add butter; still stirring, boil 3 minutes more. Remove from heat and stir in pectin and a few drops of coloring, if desired.

Pour into prepared pan and allow to set overnight in cool place. Cut into attractive shapes and roll in sugar. Store in a cool place in airtight containers with wax paper separating the layers. Will keep up to 1 week.

Makes about 2 lb.

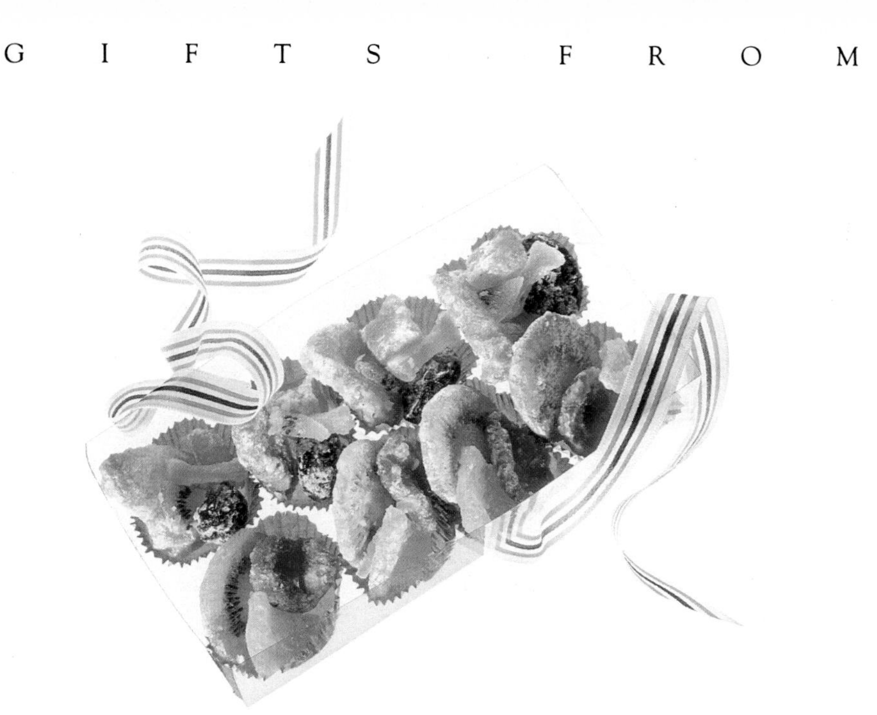

SPICED DRIED FRUIT

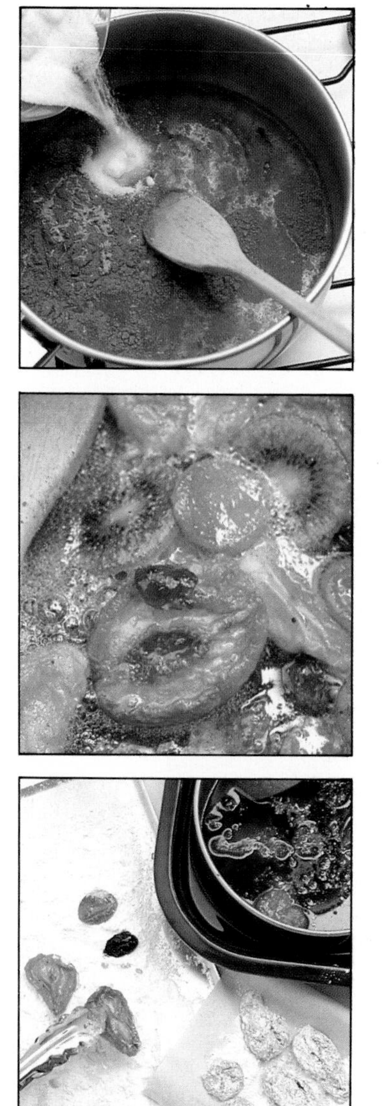

1 cup sugar
1½ teaspoons grated lemon peel
1 teaspoon powdered cinnamon
¼ teaspoon powdered cloves
¼ teaspoon powdered nutmeg
¾ cup water
5 oz dried apricots, pears or apples
Powdered sugar

In a saucepan, combine sugar, lemon peel, spices and water. Cook over a low heat, stirring constantly, until sugar dissolves. Increase the heat, bring to a boil without stirring. Boil to soft ball stage, 240F (117C) on candy thermometer.

Add fruit and cook slowly 5 minutes, stirring to avoid burning. Remove saucepan and immediately place it in a pan of warm water.

Using a fork, carefully lift out individual pieces of fruit, draining them over the pan. Roll fruit pieces immediately in powdered sugar. Package in jars or decorative boxes.

Makes about ½ lb.

APRICOT BALLS

½ cup dried apricots, chopped
½ cup pitted prunes, chopped
¼ cup raisins, chopped
3 tablespoons Cointreau or other orange liqueur
2 teaspoons grated orange peel
1⅓ cup shredded coconut
¾ cup chopped walnuts
¾ cup sugar

In a bowl, combine apricots, prunes and raisins, sprinkle with Cointreau. Allow fruit to macerate at room temperature 1 hour, stirring occasionally.

In a food processor or blender, finely chop the fruit. In a bowl, combine chopped fruit, grated orange peel, ⅔ cup coconut and walnuts; mix thoroughly.

On a plate combine sugar and remaining coconut. Form fruit mixture into small, bite-size balls and roll in sugar and coconut mixture. Store in an airtight container with wax paper between layers.

Makes 24 to 30 balls.

RUM BALLS

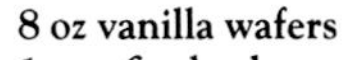

8 oz vanilla wafers
1 cup finely chopped mixed dried fruit, such as raisins, apricots, prunes, figs or dates
1 (14 oz.) can sweetened condensed milk
3 cups unsweetened shredded coconut
Grated peel of 1 lemon
2 tablespoons lemon juice
1 tablespoon unsweetened cocoa powder
2 tablespoons dark rum

In a food processor or blender, finely crush the wafers.

In a large bowl combine vanilla wafers, mixed dried fruit, condensed milk, 1 cup of coconut, lemon peel and juice, cocoa and rum.

With wet hands shape mixture into 1¼-inch balls and roll in remaining 2 cups of shredded coconut. Store in airtight containers in the refrigerator.

Makes about 45 confections.

SUGARED ORANGE PEEL

5 oranges
3 cups sugar
3 tablespoons light corn syrup
1 1/4 cups water

Quarter oranges, remove pulp and scrape white pith from peel. Cut quarters (which are now just skins) into 1/2-in strips. In a saucepan, cover peel with water. Bring to boil. Simmer 10 minutes and drain. Repeat process two more times.

In a heavy-bottomed saucepan bring 2 1/2 cups of sugar, corn syrup and water to boil over a low heat, until sugar is dissolved. Cook 20 minutes, washing down any sugar crystals adhering to sides with a brush dipped in water. Add peel; continue simmering 15 minutes more, stirring to prevent sticking. Allow syrup to be almost completely absorbed by peel, making sure it doesn't burn.

Line 2 cookie sheets with wax paper. Cover with remaining 1/2 cup sugar. Using a fork lift individual pieces of peel from pan and roll in sugar, coating peel well. Leave peel in single layer on cookie sheets overnight. Store in an airtight container, separating each layer with wax paper.

Makes about 1/2 lb.

Marzipan Fruits

1 1/4 cups finely ground almonds
3/4 cup powdered sugar (or more, if a sweeter flavor is desired)
1 egg white
Red, green, blue and yellow food coloring
A few cloves

In a heatproof bowl or top of a double boiler placed over a saucepan of hot-water, place almonds; heat gently stirring occasionally until warmed. Remove double boiler from heat, add sugar and egg white.

On a work surface, knead almond mixture until a smooth, fairly dry paste. Roll into a ball, cover with a cloth and let stand at room temperature for 15 minutes.

Break off small portions and shape into desired 'fruit'. The exact size of the fruit is up to you, but they should never be larger than a small walnut. You will need a couple of fine-pointed brushes, a saucer for mixing colors, a cup of water and a cloth for wiping brushes between color changes. Remember, red and yellow make orange, diluted orange will put the base color on peaches, red and green make brown for the stripes on bananas. Use cloves for the stem ends of oranges, pears and apples. You may make leaves from marzipan or use angelica.

Makes about 1/2 lb.

CARAMELIZED FRUITS

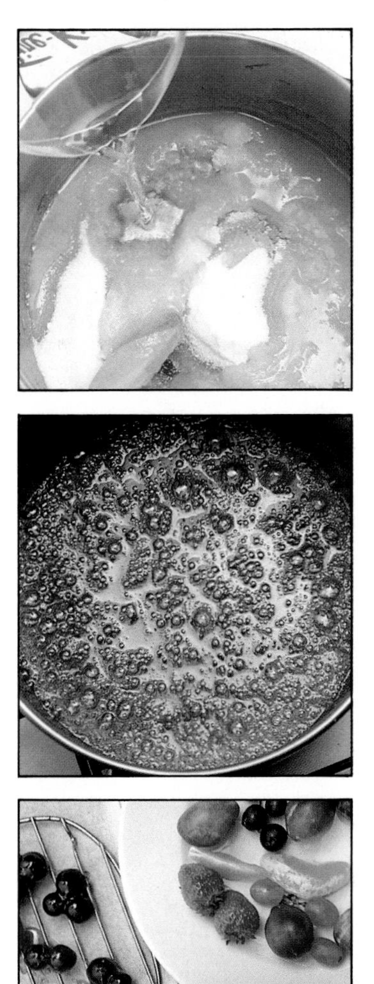

⅔ cup sugar
5 tablespoons water
Warm water
About 2 cups fresh assorted fruit, such as grapes. tangerine sections and strawberries, rinsed if necessary

In a heavy-bottomed saucepan combine sugar and water. Cook over a gentle heat, stirring occasionally until sugar is dissolved.

Bring to boil without stirring; boil until mixture turns a pale caramel color. Remove immediately from heat; place in a bowl of warm water.

Carefully place individual pieces of fruit in caramel; coating completely. Set fruit onto lightly greased cookie sheet or wire rack. Allow to cool and harden. To serve, place in petit four cases. Fruit must be eaten within 24 hours. Do not refrigerate.

Makes about 1½ lbs.

Chocolate Dipped Strawberries

20 to 25 strawberries, washed and dried, leaves intact
6 oz. semi-sweet or bittersweet chocolate, chopped
2 teaspoons vegetable shortening

In a bowl or top of a double boiler set over a pan of simmering water, melt chocolate and shortening together over very low heat. Remove from heat.

Dip bottom half of each strawberry into chocolate mixture. Rest on wax paper until set.

Place in paper cups. Store, covered, in the refrigerator.

Makes 20 to 25 strawberries.

— Chocolate Covered Prunes —

12 whole pitted prunes
12 whole Brazil nuts
8 oz semi-sweet or bittersweet chocolate, chopped

Fill cavity of prunes with Brazil nuts.

In a heatproof bowl or top of a double boiler placed over a saucepan of hot water, melt the chocolate, stirring.

Dip prunes into chocolate. Place on wax paper to set. Store, covered, in the refrigerator.

Makes 12 chocolates.

LEMON DROPS

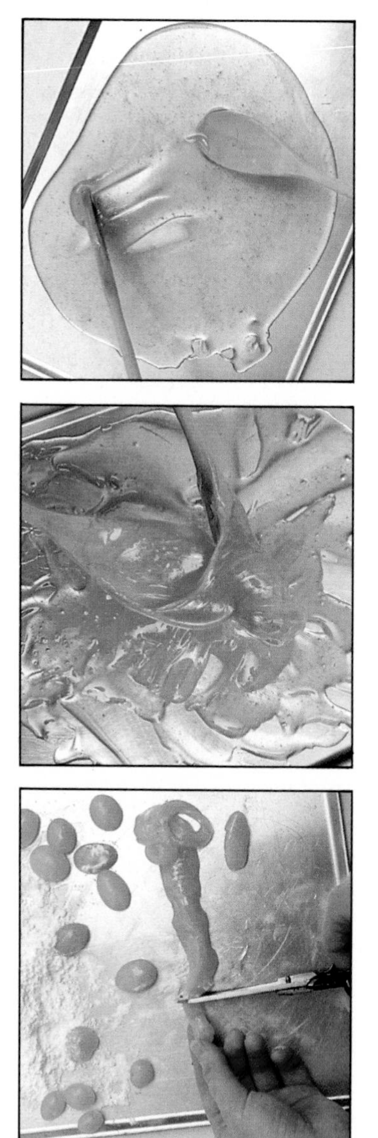

½ cup water
1⅓ cups sugar
¼ teaspoon cream of tartar
½ teaspoon lemon extract
Powdered sugar

In a large heavy-bottomed saucepan, combine water and sugar, cook over medium heat stirring to dissolve sugar. Bring to boil. Add cream of tartar and continue boiling until syrup reaches soft crack stage, 270F (140C) on candy thermometer. Remove immediately from heat – syrup should stay a pale yellow color. Add lemon extract and tartaric acid. Pour syrup onto an oiled slab or into a dish.

Using two wooden spoons, work into a toffee. Continue working until toffee becomes cool enough to handle with oiled hands. Pull toffee into a long roll.

With oiled scissors, cut off small pieces and shape with your hands into drops. Coat with powdered sugar and allow the drops to cool and dry thoroughly. Store in airtight containers.

Makes about ½ lb.

Toffee Apples

2¼ cups sugar
½ cup butter
2 tablespoons white wine vinegar
2 tablespoons boiling water
Red food coloring, if desired
Hot water
8 medium-size, crisp apples, washed, dried, skewered from top with 8 wooden Popsickle sticks or skewers
Iced water

In a heavy-bottomed saucepan, combine sugar, butter, vinegar, boiling water and a few drops of red food coloring, if desired. Cook over low heat, stirring, until sugar is dissolved. Increase heat and boil, without stirring, until mixture reaches hard crack stage, 290F (147C) on candy thermometer or using a spoon, drop a little toffee into a small bowl of cold water to test for doneness.

Place saucepan in a larger saucepan of hot water to keep toffee soft. Quickly dip apples in toffee mixture; repeat for a thicker coating.

Dip coated apples into iced water to harden the toffee. Stand on wax paper to cool. Wrap toffee apples in plastic wrap.

Makes 8 toffee apples.

NUT TOFFEES

2 cups sugar
½ cup butter, chopped
2 tablespoons white vinegar
2 tablespoons boiling water
Assortment of unsalted nuts, such as pecans, almonds, walnuts and pistachio nuts

In a heavy-bottomed saucepan, combine sugar, butter, vinegar and boiling water. Place over a low heat and stir until sugar is dissolved. Increase the heat; cook without stirring until mixture changes color. Start testing by spooning mixture by drops into a small bowl of iced water. When a firm ball is produced (test by feeling), toffee is done. Or cook to 290F (147C) on candy thermometer.

Pour into a well-buttered 9-inch square pan. Let cool.

Mark into pieces with a sharp knife. Place nuts in each square. Let cool completely and harden. Turn out onto a wooden board and break into pieces. Wrap in foil or plastic wrap.

Makes about 1 lb.

MIXED TOFFEES

4½ cups sugar
1 cup butter
¼ cup white vinegar
4 tablespoons boiling water
Glacé cherries and nuts, for decoration

In a large heavy-bottomed saucepan, bring sugar, butter, vinegar and water to a boil.

Boil until the color changes and then start testing by dropping the mixture by drops into a teacup or glass of iced water. When a firm ball is produced (test by feeling) toffee is done. Or cook to 290F (147C) on candy thermometer. Spoon immediately into small candy molds.

Decorate with cherries and nuts.

Makes about 24.

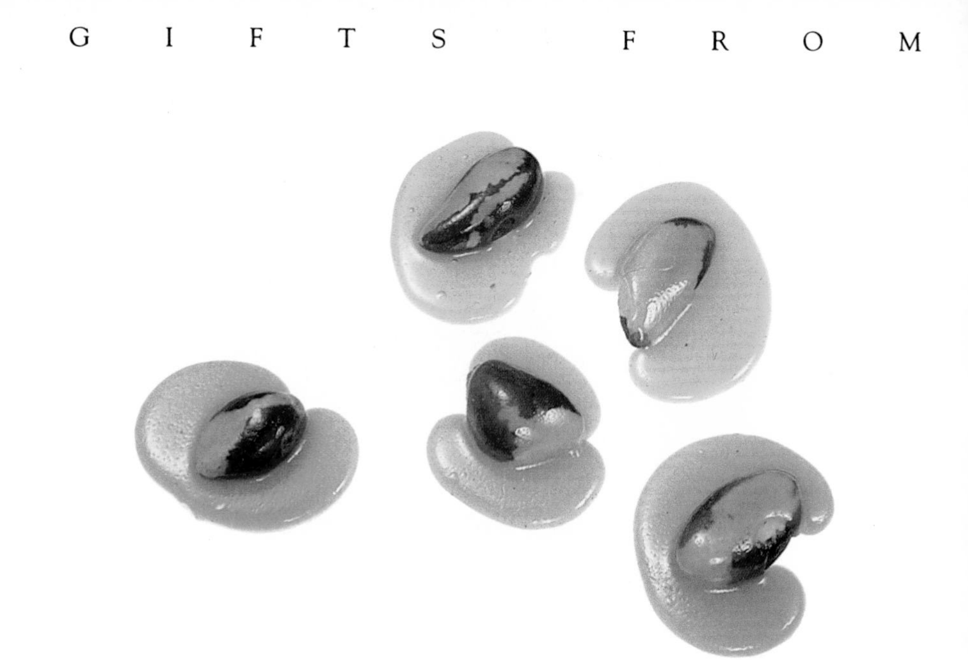

Buttered Brazil Nuts

½ to ¾ cup whole Brazil nuts
⅓ cup water
1 cup brown sugar
1½ teaspoons light corn syrup
1¼ teaspoons cream of tartar
¼ cup butter, chopped

Preheat oven to 225F (110C). On an oiled cookie sheet spread nuts in a single layer. Warm in the oven for 5-10 minutes while preparing the toffee mixture.

In a heavy-bottomed saucepan, combine water and sugar. Cook over low heat until sugar is dissolved. Bring liquid to boil, add syrup, cream of tartar and butter, simmer until butter has melted. Bring to a boil and boil to soft crack stage, 270F (140C) on candy thermometer.

Remove saucepan from heat. Remove nuts from oven. With a spoon, drizzle a little toffee over each nut. Leave to cool and harden. If toffee is setting too quickly in the pan, place it in a bowl of hot water. Store in a cool, dark place.

Makes about ½ lb.

CHOCOLATE LOGS

¼ cup finely chopped mixed candied peel
⅓ cup raisins, coarsely chopped
½ cup chopped almonds
2 tablespoons minced preserved ginger
2 tablespoons chopped walnuts
1 tablespoon sugar
⅔ cup shredded coconut
13 oz semi-sweet or bittersweet chocolate
½ cup dark or light rum
Powdered sugar

In a large bowl, combine candied peel, raisins, almonds, ginger, walnuts, sugar and coconut, set aside. Melt 5 oz chocolate in top of double boiler taking care not to let the water boil, so it doesn't get too warm.

Mix chocolate with dry ingredients; add the rum. Let cool slightly. On a surface lightly coated with powdered sugar shape chocolate mixture into finger-sized logs. Refrigerate until firm.

Melt remaining chocolate; let cool slightly. Dip cold logs in warm chocolate, covering each one thoroughly. Place on wax paper. With a fork draw lines over the warm chocolate, to resemble bark. Let set at room temperature. Wrap in cellophane or plastic wrap. Box several logs together. Store in a cool place or the refrigerator.

Makes about 2 lb.

EASY CHOCOLATE FUDGE

½ cup butter
½ cup sugar
2 tablespoons unsweetened cocoa powder
2 tablespoons shredded coconut
½ cup chopped walnuts
⅓ cup chopped glacé cherries
½ cup chopped crystallized ginger
1 tablespoon grated orange peel
½ teaspoon vanilla extract
2 cups crushed vanilla wafers
1 egg, beaten

CHOCOLATE ICING:

1 cup powdered sugar
2 tablespoons unsweetened cocoa powder
1 tablespoon butter, softened
2 tablespoons water

In a heavy-bottomed saucepan, combine butter, sugar, and cocoa. Cook, stirring occasionally, over low heat until butter melts and sugar is dissolved.

Remove from heat and stir in coconut, walnuts, cherries, ginger, orange peel, vanilla, crushed wafers and egg. Mix well and press mixture into an oiled or greased 8 x 9-in cake pan.

Sift powdered sugar and cocoa for the icing into a bowl. Add butter and water. Beat until smooth. Spread icing over fudge. Cut into pieces. Store in an airtight container.

Makes about 1 lb.

Mocha Nut Fudge

2¼ cups sugar
1¼ cups whipping cream
¼ cups butter, chopped
⅔ cup strong black coffee
8 oz. bittersweet chocolate, coarsely chopped
1 cup chopped Brazil nuts, hazelnuts or walnuts

In a heavy-bottomed saucepan over a low heat, combine sugar, cream, butter and coffee. Cook, stirring occasionally until sugar dissolves. Add chocolate to sugar mixture. Raise heat and bring to a boil, stirring frequently.

Allow mixture to reach softball stage 234F (114C) on candy thermometer. Stir in nuts.

Remove from heat and beat fudge until it begins to thicken. Immediately pour out into an oiled 8-inch baking pan. Let fudge cool, cut into squares. Wrap individual pieces in plastic wrap.

Makes about 2 lb.

Chocolate Truffles

1/3 cup sliced almonds
1/3 cup sugar
1 1/2 lbs semi-sweet or bittersweet chocolate, chopped
1 tablespoon strong coffee
1/3 cup butter, softened
2 tablespoons whipping cream
2 liqueurs of your choice
Dutch processed cocoa powder

In a small heavy-bottomed pan, combine almonds and sugar. On a low heat, slowly cook until golden brown, stirring with a wooden spoon. Remove from heat immediately and pour mixture onto an oiled plate. Allow to harden. In a food processor or blender, crush nut mixture to a coarse powder.

Melt 8 oz chocolate in a bowl or top of a double boiler set over a pan of simmering water. Stir in coffee; cool slightly. Beat in butter; stir in cream and crushed nut mixture. Divide mixture in half, flavor each half with 1 or 2 tablespoons of liqueur.

Gently roll heaping teaspoons of truffle mixture into balls. Work quickly as chocolate sets fast. Set aside on wax paper; refrigerate until firm. Melt remaining chocolate; dip some truffles and place on wax paper to set. Roll others in cocoa when almost set. Place in paper cups. Store, covered, in a cool place.

Makes about 1 1/2 lb

— Chocolate Liqueur Shells —

3 oz each of semi-sweet or bittersweet, milk and white chocolate, melted in separate bowls

Mousse:
3 oz white chocolate, chopped
2 eggs, separated
1 tablespoon each of Tia Maria, crème de menthe or Cointreau
Food coloring if desired

With a spoon, smear melted chocolate evenly over inside of 12 paper cups. Turn cups upside down on a plate. Refrigerate until set. Gently peel off the paper.

Mousse:
Slowly melt white chocolate. Remove from heat; quickly beat in egg yolks. Set aside. In a separate bowl, beat egg whites until stiff, but not dry. Divide egg yolk mix into three separate bowls and add 1 teaspoon of a different liqueur to each bowl. Add a drop or two of green food coloring to bowl containing crème de menthe – if desired. A drop or two of yellow coloring can be added to Cointreau mixture. Gently fold a third of the egg whites into each of the bowls.

Spoon into chocolate shells. Refrigerate 2 hours. These shells should be consumed within 24 hours. The chocolate cases can be made ahead of time and stored in a cool, dry place.

Makes 12 candies.

Ice Cream Easter Eggs

2 lb. chocolate, semi-sweetened or bittersweet, chopped
(quick alternative: carefully slice in half 4 purchased hollow chocolate eggs)

Egg White Filling:

4 oz white chocolate
¼ cup whipping cream
2 eggs, room temperature
2 tablespoons sugar
½ teaspoon vanilla extract

Egg Yolk Filling:

1¼ cups milk
1 egg yolk
1 tablespoon sugar
1 tablespoon cornstarch
2 tablespoons chopped almonds
4 dried apricots, finely chopped
2 teaspoons brandy
few drops yellow food coloring
4 oz semi-sweet or bittersweet chocolate, chopped, for assembling eggs and decoration
candied flowers for decoration

Egg Shells:

In the top of a double boiler or heatproof bowl placed over a saucepan of hot water, place chocolate. Place pan over a moderate heat until chocolate melts, stirring occasionally. Spread a thin layer of chocolate inside molds. Place molds open side down on a flat surface and refrigerate until firm.

Egg White Filling:

Melt white chocolate and set aside to cool. Beat cream until soft peaks form, set aside. Beat eggs with sugar and vanilla until thick and creamy. Place egg mixture on top of double boiler. Place over simmering water, cook, stirring, until mixture thickens; cool to room temperature. Stir in white chocolate until the mixture is smooth. Cool. Fold in whipped cream. Pour into trays. Freeze until almost completely frozen.

Egg Yolk Filling:
In a bowl, combine almonds, chopped apricots and brandy. Allow to stand at room temperature for 30 minutes. In a small saucepan, make a paste with cornstarch and a little milk. Beat in remaining milk, egg yolk and sugar. Bring to a simmer and stir until thickened. Add a few drops of yellow food coloring. Combine custard mixture with apricot mixture. Cool. Place in freezer until almost completely frozen.

To assemble chocolate eggs, spoon semi-frozen 'egg-white filling' into each of the chocolate egg shells. Make an indentation with the back of a spoon in the center of each egg (this is to make room for the 'yolk'.) Roll egg yolk filling into 4 balls and place in only four of the egg halves.

Melt 4 ounces chocolate and, with a warm knife or skewer, run melted chocolate over edges of eggs. Gently press egg shells together, making sure you have one half with the yolk and the other hollow.

Freeze overnight. Decorate with piped names and candied flowers.

Makes 4 eggs.

Herb Muffins

1½ cups all-purpose flour, sifted
2 tablespoons sugar
1 tablespoon baking powder
Pinch of salt
1 egg
½ cup milk
2 tablespoons butter, melted
1 cup lightly packed, fresh herbs (parsley, thyme, oregano, or sage), finely chopped

Preheat oven to 375F (190C). Sift flour, sugar, baking powder and salt together. Set aside. Beat egg and milk together, add melted butter.

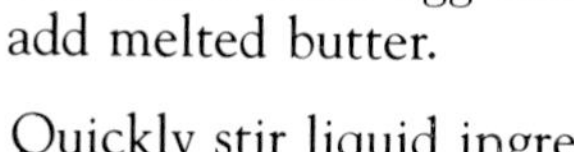

Quickly stir liquid ingredients into flour until just moistened.

Mix in herbs. Pour into greased muffin pans. Bake 15 to 20 minutes or until toothpick inserted in center comes out clean. Turn out onto wire rack to cool.

Makes 12 muffins.

Raisin Bran Muffins

1 1/4 cups all-purpose flour
1 teaspoon baking powder
1 teaspoon baking soda
Pinch of salt
1/2 cup bran
1/4 cup sugar
1 cup milk
1/2 cup raisins
1 tablespoon light corn syrup
1/4 cup butter

Preheat oven to 425F (220C). Sift flour, baking powder, baking soda and salt together; add bran and sugar.

In a saucepan warm milk, raisins, light corn syrup and butter together until butter melts. Pour mixture into dry ingredients; stir until just moistened.

Spoon into greased muffin pans. Bake 12 to 15 minutes, or until toothpick inserted into center of muffin comes out clean. Turn onto a wire rack to cool.

Makes 12 muffins.

Scottish Shortbread

1 cup butter, softened
½ cup superfine sugar
¼ cup rice flour, sifted
2⅔ cups all-purpose flour, sifted

Preheat oven to 300F (150C). Cream butter and sugar together.

Stir in flours; use your hands as mixture becomes too stiff to work with a spoon. On a lightly floured surface, knead mixture until smooth.

Gently press to desired thickness (this mixture does not roll). Cut into shapes, or use a shortbread mold (dusted with cornstarch to make unmolding easier). Or, take portions of dough and press into baking pans such as pie plates, or 8-inch square baking pans. Bake about 1 hour or until just beginning to turn golden. Turn out onto a wire rack to cool. Store in an air tight container. The quantity of shortbread this recipe yields depends upon the thickness and size you choose to make the shortbread.

MUESLI BARS

½ cup butter, chopped
¼ cup peanut butter
½ cup honey
1 cup packed brown sugar
2 cups rolled oats
1 cup puffed rice cereal
1 cup bran flakes
½ cup all-bran cereal
½ cup wheatgerm
½ cup unsweetened shredded coconut
¼ cup sesame seeds
½ cup sunflower seeds
½ cup pumpkin seeds
½ cup pine nuts
½ cup dried apricots, chopped

Heat butter, peanut butter, honey and sugar in a large heavy-bottomed skillet until butter melts and sugar dissolves. Stir occasionally to blend.

Add remaining ingredients. Cook 10 minutes, or until golden brown, stirring to prevent burning.

Turn into 9 x 13-inch greased baking dish. Press mixture lightly. Allow to cool. Cut into bars, wrap in foil or plastic wrap. Store in a cool place in an airtight container.

Makes about 35 bars.

CHOCOLATE FINGERS

1 cup powdered sugar
1 cup powdered milk
3 tablespoons unsweetened cocoa powder
⅓ cup raisins
⅓ cup glacé cherries
⅓ cup mixed candied peel
Vanilla extract
1 cup vegetable shortening, melted

Sift powdered sugar, powdered milk and cocoa into a bowl. Add fruit and toss until fruit is well coated.

Stir in shortening and a few drops of vanilla. Mix thoroughly.

Line an 8-inch square pan with plastic wrap. Pour mixture into pan. Refrigerate until firm. Turn out onto a board and cut into fingers. Wrap pieces in foil or plastic wrap. Store in an airtight container in a cool place.

Makes about 32 fingers.

GINGER COOKIES

½ cup butter, chopped
¼ cup dark corn syrup
½ cup sugar
2 cups all-purpose flour
1 tablespoon powdered ginger
1 teaspoon baking soda

LEMON GLACÉ ICING:
1¾ cups powdered sugar
juice of 1 lemon, strained, warmed
1 teaspoon butter

Preheat oven to 375F (190C). In a bowl placed over a saucepan of hot water, place butter, dark corn syrup and sugar. Stir until butter is melted and sugar is dissolved.

Sift flour, ginger and baking soda. Stir into warmed mixture until a stiff dough is formed. Wrap in plastic wrap and refrigerate 20 minutes.

On a floured board roll out to ⅛-in thickness and cut into 2-in rounds. Place on greased cookie sheet and bake 15 to 20 minutes, or until lightly browned. Cool on a wire rack.

Icing:
Sift powdered sugar into a small bowl. Stir in lemon juice and butter until smooth. Spread icing onto cold cookies.

Makes about 30 cookies.

- RASPBERRY HAZELNUT COOKIES -

½ cup butter
⅓ cup sugar
¾ cup ground hazelnuts
1 teaspoon lemon juice
1 teaspoon vanilla extract
1¼ cups all-purpose flour, sifted

RASPBERRY GLACÉ ICING:

1½ cups powdered sugar
1 teaspoon butter
1 to 2 teapoons raspberry liqueur
1½ tablespoons hot water

Preheat over to 325F (165C). Cream together butter and sugar until light and fluffy.

Stir in hazelnuts, lemon juice and vanilla. Mix in flour to form a firm dough.

On a floured board, roll out to ⅛-inch thickness and cut into 2-inch rounds. Place on greased cookie sheet and bake 10 to 15 minutes, or until lightly browned. Cool on wire rack.

Icing:
Sift powdered sugar into a bowl; add butter and raspberry liqueur. Stir in 1½ tablespoons hot water, drop by drop, until mixture is of spreading consistency. You may not need all the water. Spread icing onto completely cooled cookies.

Makes about 30 cookies.

Walnut And Chocolate Cookies

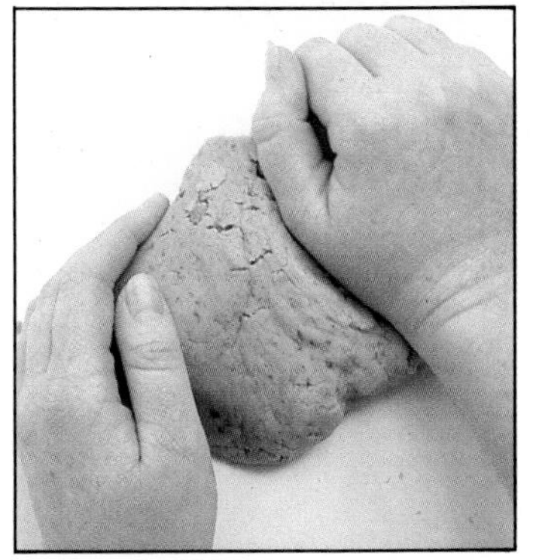

1 cup all-purpose flour
½ cup powdered sugar
½ teaspoon powdered cinnamon
½ cup butter, chopped
1 cup ground walnuts
1 teaspoon grated lemon peel
1 egg yolk, beaten

CHOCOLATE ICING:

2 oz semi-sweetened or bitter sweet chocolate
½ teaspoon vegetable shortening

Preheat oven to 325F (165C). Sift flour, powdered sugar and cinnamon together into a bowl. Cut in butter until mixture resembles coarse meal. Stir in ground walnuts, lemon peel and egg yolk.

Turn mixture onto floured board and knead until smooth. Roll out on a floured board ⅛-inch thickness and cut into 2-inch rounds. Place on a greased cookie sheet and bake 10 to 15 minutes, or until lightly browned. Cool on a wire rack.

Icing:
In double boiler very slowly melt chocolate and shortening over warm water. Dip half of each cookie into melted chocolate mixture. Refrigerate on wax paper until chocolate is set.

Makes about 40 cookies.

BRANDY SNAP BASKETS

¼ cup butter, chopped
¼ cup sugar
2 tablespoons dark corn syrup
½ cup all-purpose flour
½ teaspoon powdered ginger
1 teaspoon brandy or rum flavoring

Preheat oven to 350F (175C). Cut nine 6 x 6-inch squares of baking parchment. In a saucepan combine butter, sugar and syrup; cook over a low heat until butter melts. Sift flour and ginger together. Stir into butter mixture. Add brandy flavoring and mix well.

Place baking parchment on cookie sheets. Drop a tablespoon of batter onto center of each parchment square. Bake 7 minutes, or until the cookies are a dark golden brown.

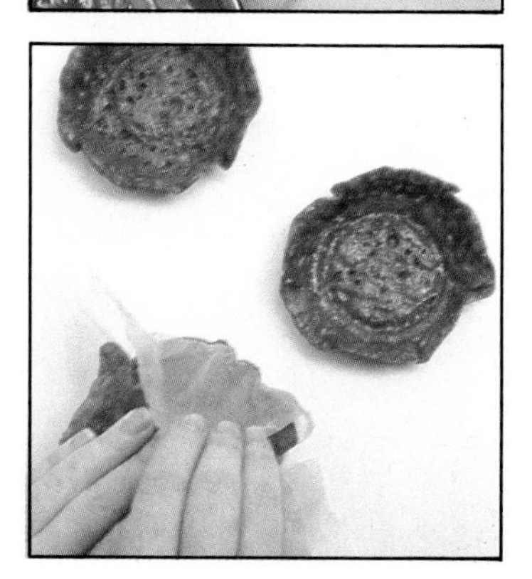

Remove from oven and let rest for a minute. Place cookies over the base of inverted lightly greased glasses and gently peel off paper. Allow to cool. To serve, fill with ice cream, whipped cream, and/or fresh fruit. Store, unfilled, in an air-tight container.

Makes about 9.

FLORENTINES

¼ cup unsalted butter
⅓ cup packed brown sugar
2 tablespoons all-purpose flour, sifted
¼ cup finely chopped walnuts
¼ cup sliced almonds
¼ cup finely chopped hazelnuts
1 tablespoon finely chopped glacé cherries
2 tablespoons finely chopped mixed candied peel
4 oz semi-sweet or bittersweet chocolate
1 teaspoon vegetable shortening

Preheat oven to 350F (175C). Cream butter and sugar together until fluffy. Mix in flour; stir in nuts, cherries and candied peel. Drop mixture by tablespoons onto greased cookie sheets leaving 4 to 5 inches between each cookie (batter spreads as it bakes).

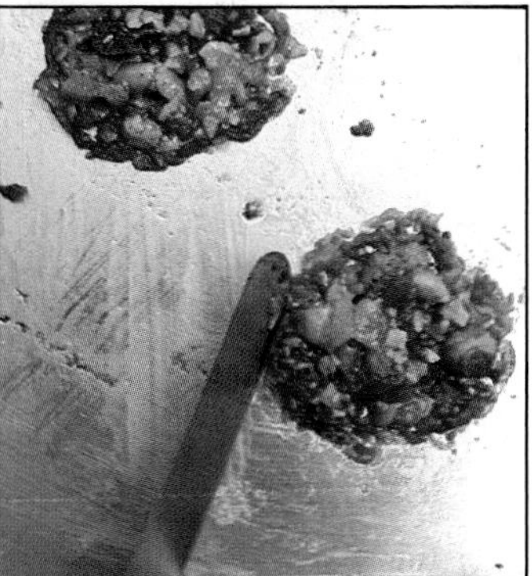

Bake 4 minutes or until cookies are golden brown. Allow to rest for a minute before removing onto a wire rack to firm and cool.

In a double boiler, slowly melt chocolate with vegetable shortening. Spread chocolate over smooth underside of cookie and, with a fork, score the chocolate in waves. Refrigerate until set. Store in an airtight container in a cool place.

Makes about 30.

Chocolate Boxes

2 eggs, room temperature
1/4 cup sugar
1/2 cup all-purpose flour, sifted
2 tablespoons butter, melted
Orange marmalade, warmed
12 to 18 caramelized mandarin orange segments, page 85
2/3 cup whipping cream, lightly whipped
36 chocolate squares or orange flavored chocolate squares (about 2 to 3-inches square

Preheat oven to 425F (220C). Beat eggs and sugar together until pale lemon in color and thick. Fold flour alternately into egg mixture with melted butter. Pour into a greased and floured 8-in square baking pan. Bake 8 to 10 minutes or until toothpick inserted into center comes out clean before turning out on to a wire rack. Cool cake completely then cut into 1-in squares.

Lay 2 pieces of 18-in long ribbon in a cross on wax paper. Place a chocolate square over center of ribbons; brush lightly with marmalade. Top with piece of cake, brush sides of cake with marmalade. Press a chocolate square on all 4 sides of cake.

Spoon in whipped cream, top with 2 or 3 caramelized mandarin orange segments. Rest a square of chocolate, tilted slightly upward, on top as lid. Tie ribbons together in a bow. Repeat for all six boxes. Will keep up to 24 hours.

Makes 6.

PETITS FOURS

½ cup almond paste
1 cup sugar
8 eggs
1 cup butter
1 teaspoon vanilla extract
2½ cups all-purpose flour sifted with
3 teaspoons baking powder
1 lb. fondant
Almond and vanilla extract
Green, pink and yellow food colorings
Almond slivers, walnut halves, candied violets, candied fruits, for decoration

Preheat oven to 350F (175C). Blend together almond paste, ½ cup of sugar and 1 egg.

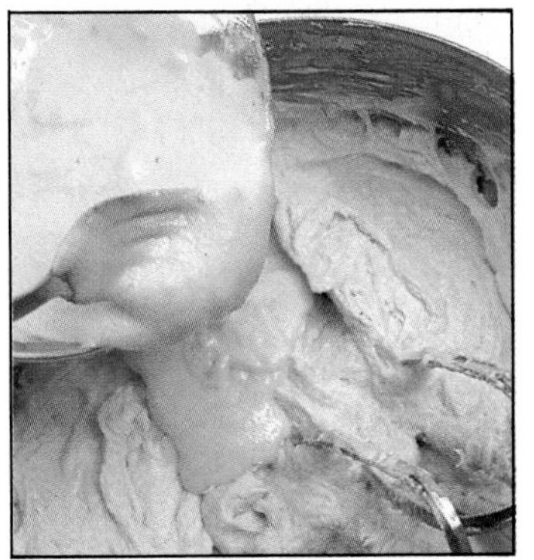

Cream butter with remaining sugar. Gradually beat in remaining eggs. then vanilla and almond mixture. Gradually fold flour into egg mixture. Spread in buttered 10 x 15-inch jelly roll pan. Bake 30 minutes. Allow to cool in pan. Cut into small squares or diamonds.

Soften fondant in a bowl set over a pan of simmering water, stirring occasionally. Pour into 3 small bowls placed in a basin of hot water. Flavor with vanilla or almond extract. Add coloring. Dip cake pieces individually into fondant. Decorate while still moist.

Makes about 40 petits fours.

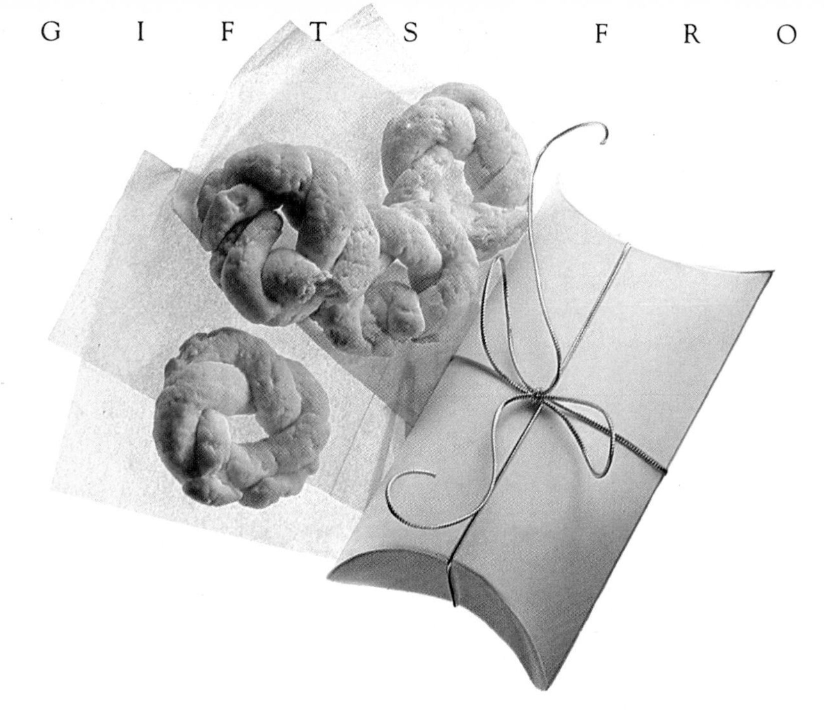

BRANDY ROPE RINGS

1 cup butter, softened
¾ cup sugar
2½ cups all-purpose flour, sifted
1 teaspoon powdered cinnamon
3 tablespoons brandy

Preheat oven to 350F (175C). Cream butter and sugar together until light and fluffy. Stir flour and cinnamon into creamed mixture. Stir in brandy and mix well.

Turn dough onto a floured board and roll to ¼-inch thickness. Cut dough into ¾ x 5-inch strips. Twist two of the strips together to form a 'rope'.

Join the two ends of the 'ropes' together to form a circle. Repeat with remaining strips. Place circles on cookie sheets lined with baking parchment. Bake 15 minutes, or until golden brown. These cookies can be left plain, drizzled with glaze, or threaded together with ribbon. They can also be hung on the Christmas tree or boxed as gifts.

Makes about 24.

MINCEMEAT TARTS

1¾ cups all-purpose flour
1 tablespoon sugar
⅔ cup butter, chopped
2 tablespoons water
1 egg yolk, beaten
Mincemeat, page 63
Powdered sugar, if desired

In a mixing bowl, combine flour and sugar. Cut in butter until mixture resembles coarse meal. Add egg yolk and water and mix into a firm dough. Wrap and refrigerate 1 hour.

Preheat oven to 375F (190C). On a floured surface, roll pastry to ⅛-inch thickness. Cut into 3-inch circles with plain or fluted edge cutter. These are for bottom crusts. For top crusts, cut dough into 1½-inch rounds with plain or fluted edge cutter. Place bottom pastry circles into muffin pans. Fill with a heaping teaspoon of mincemeat. Cover with top pastry circles.

Using a fork, pierce pastry cicles to allow steam to escape. Bake 10 minutes, or until the tarts are a light golden brown. Place on wire racks to cool. Dust with powdered sugar if desired. Store in an airtight container up to 3 days.

Makes about 10 tarts.

CHRISTMAS CRACKERS

2 tablespoons Cointreau or orange liqueur
½ cup slivered almonds
2 lb. mincemeat, page 63, or use store bought
8 sheets of filo pastry
¼ cup butter, melted
4 tablespoons dry bread crumbs
1 egg, beaten
Red and green maraschino cherries, small silver dragées (silver candy balls), for decoration

Preheat oven to 450F (230C). In a bowl, mix Cointreau, almonds and mincemeat together. Lay a sheet of pastry on a board, brush with melted butter, sprinkle with 1 tablespoon bread crumbs; cover with another sheet of pastry, brush again with butter.

Spoon ¼ of mincemeat mixture 1½-in from the long edge, leaving 3½-in from short edges. Cut short edges of the pastry using pinking shears, if desired. Roll pastry enclosing mincemeat, gently twist ends. Form 3 more rolls.

Place crackers on a baking sheet lined with baking parchment. Roll 8 small balls out of foil (about ½-in in diameter). Place a ball in each end of each cracker to hold pastry open. Brush crackers with beaten egg. Bake 10 minutes, or until pastry is golden brown. Cool on a wire rack. Decorate.

Makes 4 crackers.

CHRISTMAS GARLAND

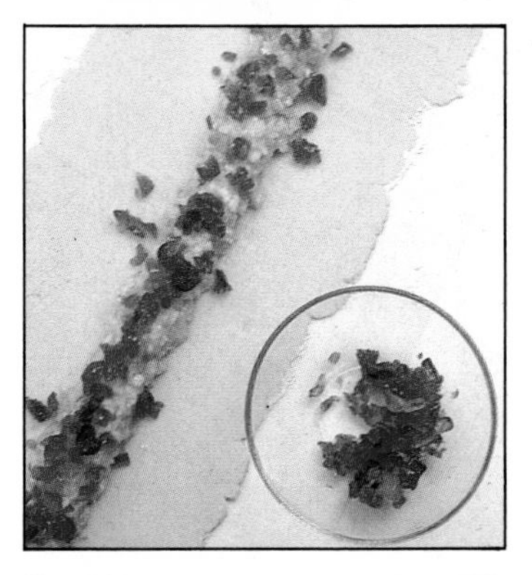

½ cup butter
1 ½ cups sifted, all-purpose flour
2 tablespoons superfine sugar
¼ cup lemon juice
1 egg yolk
2 to 4 tablespoons water
½ cup blanched almonds
⅓ cup candied lemon peel
¼ cup sugar
1 egg white
Few drops of almond extract
1 teaspoon grated lemon peel
20 red and green glacé cherries, chopped
Extra egg white for glazing
½ cup powdered sugar, sifted
2 teaspoons lemon juice, warmed
Nuts, glacé cherries and candied peel, for decoration

Cut butter into flour and sugar until mixture resembles coarse meal. Mix in lemon juice, egg yolk and enough water to form a firm dough. Wrap; refrigerate 8 hours. Roll to a large rectangle.

In a food processor or blender, combine next 6 ingredients. Cover; refrigerate 8 hours. Roll into a long sausage, place down the center of dough. Sprinkle filling with cherries. Brush edges of dough with water, fold over filling to form a roll. Press together firmly.

Shape roll into a circle, pressing the open ends together carefully. Place seam-side down on greased cookie sheet. Brush with egg white. Refrigerate 30 minutes. Preheat oven to 400F (205C). Bake 20 to 25 minutes, or until golden brown. Cool on a wire rack. In a small bowl, mix powdered sugar and lemon juice until smooth. Drizzle over garland. Decorate.

Makes 1 garland.

FRUIT CAKE

1½ cups whole Brazil nuts
2 cups walnut halves
1 cup whole blanched almonds
¾ cup mixed candied peel
¾ cup chopped pitted dates
¾ cup chopped raisins
¼ cup glacé or candied ginger
1¾ cups all-purpose flour
½ teaspoon baking powder
½ cup superfine sugar
3 eggs, lightly beaten
Few drops vanilla extract
Glacé cherries, for decoration

Preheat oven to 275F (135C). Line a buttered 9 x 5-inch loaf pan with baking parchment. Butter parchment well. Place nuts, candied peel, dates, raisins and ginger in a large bowl. Reserve some nuts to decorate top of cake. Sift together flour and baking powder. Add to fruit and nuts and mix in sugar.

Stir in eggs and vanilla until thoroughly combined. Pack into loaf pan.

Decorate top with reserved nuts and glacé cherries. Bake 2 to 2½ hours, or until toothpick inserted into center comes out clean. Allow cake to cool for ½ hour in loaf pan before turning out onto wire rack to cool completely. Store in an airtight container – will keep up to 12 months.

Makes 1 cake.

SIMNEL CAKE

2 lb. mixed dried fruit, such as raisins, apricots, prunes, figs or dates; chopped
½ cup of sherry or brandy
2 tablespoons orange marmalade
1½ cups brown sugar
5 eggs
1 cup butter, melted
2 cups self-raising flour
1 lb. marzipan* for icing

Scour and dry terracotta pots 4-4½ inches across the top. Line pots with well-buttered foil; set aside. Preheat oven to 275F (140C). In a bowl combine chopped dried fruit with sherry. Allow to marinate at room temperature for 4 hours.

Combine marinated fruit with marmalade, brown sugar, eggs, butter and flour.

Divide mixture evenly between four pots. Place all four on large cookie sheet. Bake 2 hours or until toothpick inserted into center comes out clean. Allow the cakes to cool in pots. Invert then remove foil. Roll ¼ of marzipan between two sheets of wax paper to ⅛ to ¼-inch thickness. Cover top of each cake. Roll remaining marzipan into balls. Place on top of cakes.

* in gourmet or baking section of supermarket

Makes 4 cakes.

PASSOVER NUT CAKE

4 eggs, room temperature
1 cup sugar
pinch of salt
1 lb Brazil nuts, or walnuts, finely ground
Coarsely chopped nuts for decoration

Preheat oven to 350F (175C). In a large bowl, beat together eggs, sugar and salt until they are a pale lemon color, thick and fluffy.

Fold finely ground nuts into egg mixture.

Pour into a lightly oiled 8-inch round cake pan. Decorate top with coarsely chopped nuts. Bake 45 minutes to 1 hour. Let stand 10 minutes before turning out onto a cake rack to cool completely. During Passover this cake is not iced. However, a chocolate glacé icing is nice.

Makes 1 cake.

Seeded Bread Sticks

1 tablespoon dried yeast
½ cup warm water
4 teaspoons honey
½ cup butter, chopped
1 teaspoon salt
½ cup water
1 egg, beaten
3¼ cups all-purpose flour
1 egg
Caraway, sesame and poppy seeds

In a small bowl mix together yeast, warm water and 1 teaspoon honey. Set aside and allow yeast to become foamy. In a saucepan, combine butter, remaining 3 teaspoons honey, salt and water. Heat gently until butter and honey melt. Pour liquid into large warmed bowl. Stir beaten egg and yeast into mixture.

Beat in flour. Do not knead dough. Cover and place in refrigerator until cold. Divide dough into 12 pieces. On a floured board, roll each piece to a 12-inch length. Cut in halves lengthways. Place lengths on greased cookie sheets about 4-inches apart.

In a small bowl beat remaining egg with 1 teaspoon water. Brush egg over lengths. Sprinkle with seeds. Let rise in a warm place for 30 minutes, or until not quite doubled in size. Preheat oven to 425F (220C). Bake bread sticks 15 minutes, or until golden brown. Cool on a wire rack.

Makes 24 sticks.

A selection of savory cheeses garnished with fruit. Clockwise from the top: Cheese and Walnuts, page 39; Goat Cheese in Olive Oil, page 36; Spiked Cheese Balls, page 37.

A tempting array of delicious snacks.
Stuffed Cherry Tomatoes, page 40;
Bridge Canapés, page 42.

A delightful combination for a lunch-time snack. Clockwise from the top: Seeded Bread Sticks, page 119; Pickled Mushrooms, page 26; Rillettes, page 56.

A charming array of tempting sweets.
Clockwise from the top:
Chocolate Dipped Strawberries, page 86; Chocolate Truffles, page 96; Petits Fours, page 111; Marzipan Fruits, page 84; Coffee Liqueur, page 75.

A charming combination for dessert.
Brandy Snap Basket, page 108;
Macedoine of Fruit in Brandy, page 72.

A range of savory snacks and preserves for the perfect ploughman's lunch. Clockwise from the top: Pickled Mixed Vegetables, page 24; Green Peppercorn Mustard, page 16; English Pork Pie, page 58; Olive Cheese Balls, page 38; Home Cured Pickles, page 22.

An appetizing variety of preserves and muffins. Clockwise from the top: Herb Muffins, page 100; Rum and Plum Jam, page 65; Rosemary and Quince Jelly, page 68; Apricot and Almond Conserve, page 62; Raisin Bran Muffins, page 101.

A selection of tasty appetizers. Clockwise from the top: Green Marinated Olives, page 35; Sweet Spiced Nuts, page 33; Black Marinated Olives, page 35; Mexican Peanuts, page 34.

INDEX